The Outdoors Almanac

This book is dedicated to Jacque,
Ashley, Shana, and Spring,
the ladies who have had the greatest
influence on both my career and my life.
You all contributed to the creation
of this book, and for that I thank you.

The Outdoors Almanac

Len McDougall

Burford Books

Printed in the United States of America.
Interior Design and Typesetting: Desktop Miracles, Stowe, Vermont

Library of Congress Cataloging in Publication Data

McDougall, Len.
 The outdoors almanac / Len McDougall.
  p.   cm.
 Includes index.
 ISBN 1-58080-035-1
 1. Outdoor recreation—United States.   2. Outdoor life—United States.
I. Title.
GV191.4.M34   1999
796.5—dc21

99-28384
CIP

Contents

Introduction   *vii*

1. Outfitting   1

Compasses   2
Fire-Starting Kits   5
Knives   7
Portable Water Filters   12
Footwear   14
Handwear   25
Backpacks   26
Sleeping Bags   29
Tents   34
Binoculars   37
Communications   39
Flashlights   42
Snowshoes   44
Directory of Outdoor Equipment Sources   48

2. Orienteering   53

The Basics   53
Maps   54
Advanced Orienteering   56
Night Navigation   61
Other Orienteering Tricks   61

3. Backpacking   65

Loading Up   66
Trail Hazards   68
Beating the Bugs   73

4. Making Camp   75

Selecting a Campsite   75
Campfires   76
Getting a Good Night's Sleep   79
Animals in Camp   82
Drying Wet Clothes   83
Keeping the Campsite Organized   84

5. Campsite Cooking   85

Campfire Cooking   85
Camp Foods   89
Mess Kits   91

6. Wilderness First Aid   **95**
Wilderness First-Aid Kits   97
Treating Wilderness Afflictions and Emergencies   98

7. Useful Wild Plants   **109**
Common Plantain (*Plantago major*)   110
Common Burdock (*Arctium minus*)   111
Tall Goldenrod (*Solidago altissima*)   111
Wild Leek (*Allium tricoccum*)   112
Watercress (*Nasturtium officinale*)   114
Violets (*Viola spp.*)   115
Bracken Fern (*Pteridium aquilinum*)   116
Broadleaf Cattail (*Typha latifolia*)   117
Reindeer Moss (*Cladina rangiferina*)   119
Common Jewelweed (*Impatiens capensis*)   120
Highbush Blackberry (*Rubus allegheniensis*)   122
Sweet Joe-Pye Weed (*Eupatorium purpureum*)   122
Fragrant Cudweed (*Gnaphalium obtusifolium*)   123
Catnip (*Nepeta cataria*)   125
Common Tansy (*Tanacetum vulgare*)   126

8. Survival   **129**
McDougall's Laws of Wilderness Survival   130
Shelter   130
Fire   134
The Coal Bed   136
Water   137
Food   142
Survival Knots   143
Survival Skills   146
Emergency Signals   152

9. About Animals   **155**
The Natural Order of Life in the Wild   155
Tracking Wildlife   158

10. Weather   **177**
Identifying Approaching Weather   178
Avoiding Weather Problems   180

11. Man's Rightful Place   **185**
Legend of the Red-Winged Blackbird   187
Ursa Major and Ursa Minor   191
Bearwalks   192
God's Knife   193

Index   197

Introduction

How intelligent any of us appears in any situation depends on what the topic of conversation is at the time. Plumbers make their livings at a vocation that few people give second thoughts to—at least until a drain stops up. Auto mechanics are sometimes too aware that the services listed on a repair bill are gibberish to most clients, and few homeowners would attempt to wire a 220-volt dryer outlet themselves.

My specialty is the outdoors, and never do I take for granted the blessings that came from growing up, living, and learning hard in the wild places of northern Michigan. I didn't play team sports in high school, because I was too busy hunting, fishing, and trapping to provide my family with much-needed cash and table fare, but today I believe the path I walked yielded far richer rewards.

The skills I learned from local Odawa and Ojibwa Indians who were my mentors have served me well many times. Still, I've always exhibited a real knack for getting into situations that tested my ability to stay alive. I lay alone in the woods for three days after being bitten by a rattlesnake at age 16, and nearly died in a blizzard during my first winter camping trip that same year. In 30 years of roaming the woods I've probably pulled, or at least seen, just about every self-destructive boneheaded stunt a woodsman can commit—and still lived to tell about it.

Talking about lessons learned—many of them the hard way—is the reason behind this book. This isn't a survival manual in the conventional sense, but rather a handbook of skills and techniques, salted here and there with meaningful anecdotes, that have proved most useful to outdoorsmen of every discipline. There has never been a really comprehensive encyclopedia of wilderness tips and techniques; this book is intended to fill that niche for a handy reference that works as well in a tacklebox or backpack as it does on a bookshelf. From its pages an outdoorsman can preview what to expect from a given environment under a variety of conditions. By knowing what to bring with you, what to expect, and how to react when stuff happens, your visits to the wilderness will go more smoothly, and everyone will have more fun.

I have a personal reason for writing this book as well. At least two generations have now grown up regarding the wilderness as an inhospitable and dangerous place, where any camper gone missing for 72 hours is presumed dead, and just venturing off the beaten track can become an adventure. We humans have quite literally become aliens on our own planet. Maybe passing along the lessons I've learned—and seen others learn—in three decades can help make the wilderness seem less intimidating, so that its visitors can appreciate more freely the miracles of nature that surround them. I don't see how anyone can gain a familiarity with the natural world without also falling in love with it. Being secluded deep in the woods for a few days has miraculous healing effects on body and soul, forcing the most nagging problem to assume proper insignificance. And if more people learn to love and respect our remaining wilderness areas, the voices raised in their defense will be that much louder and harder to ignore.

1

Outfitting

I was 16 the first time I tried my hand at winter camping, and it was a learning experience I'm not likely to forget. I'd purposely selected a warm March day, with temperatures hovering at the freezing mark, to begin my trip. But God has a special sense of humor where fools, drunks, and woodsmen are concerned.

I awoke at 6 A.M. the following morning when my mountain tent collapsed under more than a foot of fresh, wind-driven snow. My transistor AM radio—tuned to WJML, the only local station on the air in those days—informed me that temperatures had fallen to -20 degrees Fahrenheit, discounting windchill. The 6 miles between camp and home had turned to hostile wasteland overnight.

My leather boots and gloves, wet from the previous day, were frozen hard; my sleeping bag was woefully inadequate; and, most serious, my simple fire-starting kit just didn't work under these harsh conditions. I escaped with no more than severe frostbite and a good dose of hypothermia by abandoning my gear and walking home, half frozen, humbled, and keenly aware of my own insignificance in the natural world.

Twenty-two years later I rolled out of a sleeping bag at about the same hour to worse weather in even more remote country. Again a foot of fresh snow covered the ground, with the ambient temperature sitting at -20, and windchills, according to my Grundig AM-FM-shortwave receiver, at below -60. An excited local newsman announced that every road in the state was officially closed to motorists, and that snowplows had been recalled to wait out the storm. I pulled on my pac-boots, started a fire, and made a hot breakfast without so much as catching a chill.

Two decades of experience notwithstanding, the real difference between those two outings lay with the equipment I had with me each time. The quality and innovation that goes into outdoor gear technology increases every year. Today's equipment can accommodate any environment on the planet.

But selecting the tools best suited to your needs can be a frustrating chore. There's an awful lot of stuff on the outdoor market today, most of it good to excellent, but deciding which items are necessary—or even useful—in a given environment can cause real confusion. Nor can you always count on advice from salesclerks at the local outfitter or sporting goods store, because often they'll know less than you do.

This section is intended to serve as a buyer's guide for outdoor lovers of every discipline. Dozens of gear manufacturers contributed advice and merchandise to this compilation. Every product recommended here has been thoroughly field-tested in harsher conditions than most outdoorsmen are likely to face, because when you're in the boondocks, there's no acceptable explanation for equipment failure.

Compasses

If you want to see nature and its inhabitants at their wildest and finest, you have to leave the beaten track, because many animals, especially predators, shun humans. There's a magical quality about standing on soil that probably no one alive has seen, but before you go, understand this: Our species does not possess the instinctive sense of direction common to "lower" animals, and probably never did. The magnetic deposit that serves as a compass in the muzzles and beaks of other animals is present in our noses, too, but it doesn't work, and I've seen this proved many times.

A well-made compass is a vital component of every backcountry hiking kit—I generally carry two. Global Positioning System (GPS) units that use microwave satellite signals to triangulate the user's position to within 100 yards are impressive, but they cannot replace a compass. A good compass is found in only two states: Either it points to the magnetic north pole all the time, every day, forever, or it's damaged. The only exception to this rule occurs if the unit's magnetic needle is drawn toward a nearby metal object or deflected by iron deposits in mountain country, and both of those situations are usually obvious from the way the needle moves.

Probably most sporting compasses made today are adequate, and a few are outstanding, but there are tests every buyer should make before reaching for his wallet. First, the compass capsule should be liquid filled; this gives the indicator needle a fast, smooth action and eliminates the annoying needle bounce common to many unfilled compasses.

Never purchase a liquid-filled compass that has a bubble of any size in its capsule. Small bubbles sometimes occur as the result of repeated exposure to temperature extremes, but a bubble in a new compass indicates lack of workmanship at the factory. You can count on that bubble to grow larger with time, until it physically blocks the indicator from turning and renders the instrument useless.

Held flat in the palm and parallel to the earth, as if you were taking a bearing, the compass needle should remain fixed on magnetic north, rotating smoothly as you turn completely around. Any sign of stickiness or hesitation is reason enough for rejection. There are too many inexpensive high-quality compasses out there for you to settle for second best in this vital piece of gear.

The compass I refer to most often for bearing confirmations and corrections while trekking through heavy bush and forest is a simple "pocket" compass worn around my neck. In such country, where vision might be limited to a few yards, the ability to precisely sight on a distant landmark means little, and even the most versatile compass is largely reduced to just pointing north. Pocket compasses I've liked best include Brunton USA's Tag-A-Long series, priced from $6 to $9, depending on whether or not you want a built-in thermometer, and Silva's Type 12 ($7). Accurate to within 5 degrees, nearly indestructible, and small

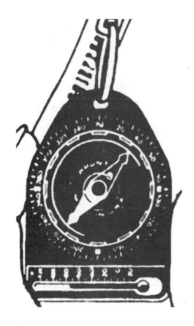

Brunton 9045 Tag-A-Long PLUS.
Courtesy Brunton USA.

enough that you can forget you're wearing one, any of these is well suited to shorter hikes of 5 miles or so.

For treks of more than 5 miles, a compass designed to work with a topographical grid map is a must. Going around mountains and lakes, crossing swollen rivers, and dodging gnarly swamps can make following a straight-line course impossible. A good topographical map (about four bucks from the United States Geological Survey; see the source list on page 52) and a compass made to exploit the information it contains are essential to anyone wanting to shortcut through untracked country.

Map compasses that have proved their worth include the Polaris from Silva ($10), Brunton's 8020 ($28) and 9020 ($12), and Suunto's M-5DL ($30). If your travels include high or open terrain that permits using faraway landmarks as bearings, prismatic sighting compasses like Brunton's 8040 ($50), the Nexus Ranger Pro ($60), and Silva's Ranger ($45) allow precise bearings to be taken from several miles distant.

Global Positioning System (GPS) units are technology's answer to the old compass and map, even though every one of these handheld satellite links is sold with a disclaimer stating that it should not be the user's only means of navigation. Having field-tested the Expedition II from Eagle Electronics for four months under a variety of conditions, I can only agree wholeheartedly. A GPS offers no real advantage over a grid map and sighting compass in the hands

Brunton 8040 Prismatic Compass. *Courtesy Brunton USA.*

of a savvy orienteer, but it does have a maximum battery life of just 20 hours, my sample lost its satellite lock repeatedly under leafless trees, and I had to carry the unit flat in my palm constantly to maintain its lock. In short a GPS can be used to augment and verify compass bearings, but a $250 GPS unit cannot yet replace a $6 compass.

The Eagle Expedition GPS.

Fire-Starting Kits

Fire has been the single greatest factor in mankind's emergence from the jungle. With it, our ancestors were able to survive earth's most hostile climes, prolong life by heating food and water to kill parasites, and create conditions that led to discoveries like pottery, smelted metal, and glass. Even today fire can have life-or-death significance to outdoorsmen on every continent—especially at night, because hypothermia can occur whenever air temperatures fall below 50 degrees Fahrenheit. Unfortunately, the need for fire increases as the conditions for starting it become less favorable, so outdoorsmen of every discipline require the means to make fire quickly in any environment, in any weather.

One fire starter that should always be carried is an ordinary disposable butane lighter, available for less than $1 in nearly every retail outlet on earth. As advertised, this ubiquitous feature of modern life is equivalent to about a thousand sulfur matches, and while it won't spark when wet, a butane lighter is no worse for wear after drying.

The Strike Force fire starter.

I've field-tested virtually every fire starter made for outdoorsmen and the military, and I can recommend only two. First is the Strike Force tool from Survival, Inc. (see the source list on page 52). Once marketed under the same name by Gerber Legendary Blades, this modern version of the frontiersman's flint-and-steel is encased in an unbreakable plastic body that measures just 5 by 1½ by 1 inches. The unit snaps apart at its center to reveal a striker in one half, and a ½-inch-diameter rare-earth flint rod in the other. Forcefully scraping the striker against the flint produces arc-welder-like sparks that can by themselves ignite most dry tinder materials. For especially harsh or wet conditions, an easily ignited, nature-friendly chemical tinder cube stored under a snap cap in the unit's butt makes it possible to start a warm fire in any weather. The Strike Force retails for about $12. Replacement tinder cubes retail for about $6 a dozen.

The other manufactured fire starter I recommend is the Blast Match, also made by Survival, Inc. This palm-size (4 by 1¼ by 1 inches), one-piece unit consists of a heavy plastic housing with an attached cap that pulls upward, allowing the spring-loaded flint rod to extend. The cap then rotates downward to nest in the bottom of the handle, out of the way. Pressing down onto the built-in striker tab with your thumb and then pushing the ½-inch flint rod forcefully against a hard surface discharges a shower of hot sparks equal to the Strike Force, except that the Blast Match requires just one hand to

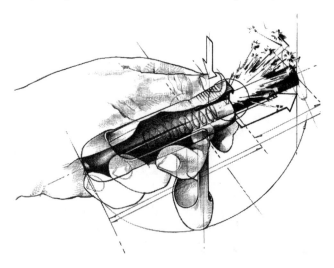

Blast Match fire starter. *Courtesy Survival, Inc.*

operate. The Blast Match doesn't carry a tinder cube (you can tuck one into a pocket), but it too has a spark hot enough to ignite most natural tinder materials. While I've found nothing to complain about in my sample, the unit isn't quite as stout as a Strike Force, though it does take up less space. But if you carry it in a pocket, I recommend rubber-banding it against accidental opening. The Blast Match retails for about $12.

Knives

Although there seems to be some sort of stigma attached to carrying a functional knife, it nonetheless remains one of the three most important tools you can have in the woods. Virtually every animal except us has been endowed by nature with implements for digging, tearing, and cutting, because these abilities are crucial to survival in a natural environment. It behooves us to follow nature's example.

The style of knife I recommend most is a fixed-blade sheath knife worn on the belt religiously, even obsessively, anytime you're not in your sleeping bag. It must be stout enough for prying, heavy enough for light chopping, and of good steel that will hold its edge, but not so large and bulky that it feels unwieldy in the hand. I prefer thoroughbred survival knives that have thick blades, a row of saw teeth along the blade spine for cutting sharp grooves in wood, a roughened handle that

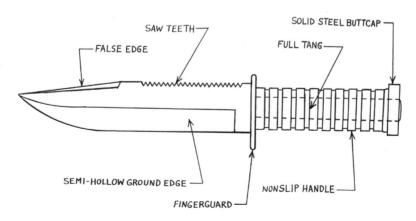

A Bowie-type survival knife is one of the most important tools you can carry in the wilderness.

won't slip when wet, and a solid buttcap for pounding. The blade's point should be on the same axis as the handle's center to make drilling holes in the fireboard of a bow-and-drill, deadfall trigger, or shelter support easy. The sheath should also be functional; many contain pockets for storing emergency items (recommended) and some even sport bottle openers, wire cutters, and screwdrivers.

I've field-tested virtually every belt knife made, and there are several I can recommend with confidence. Buck's M-9 Field Knife ($150; see the source list on page 48) is very good; its hammer-forged 7⅛-inch modified-Bowie blade of 420 stainless is virtually unbreakable, while the smartly designed Zytel sheath sports a wire cutter, bottle opener, flat screwdriver,

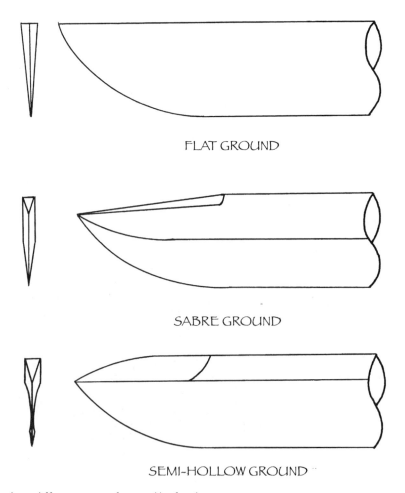

FLAT GROUND

SABRE GROUND

SEMI-HOLLOW GROUND

Three different types of survival knife edges.

and pouch large enough to hold basic survival tools. Schrade's new Extreme Survival knife ($120) has a wide stiletto-style blade, 7¼ inches long, of 440 stainless with coarse and fine saw teeth along its thick spine, a claw-hammer butt for driving and pulling nails, and two sheath pouches. Gerber's LMF (Lightweight Multi-Function) knife ($130) is the most handsome of the thoroughbred survival knives with its contoured Hypalon handle and 6-inch stainless Bowie-style blade; the heavy Cordura sheath has a strap for attaching your own storage pouch. If

The Schrade Extreme Survival knife is a fine example of a versatile and dependable belt knife. *Courtesy Schrade Cutlery*

money is a concern, Ontario Knife's legendary USAF Survival Knife with its 5½-inch 1095 carbon-steel blade and stout leather sheath remains a best buy at around $25.

(Left to Right) The Schade M7-S, Buck M9 and Gerber BMF.

I also recommend packing a working-size folding knife for cutting jobs that demand a lighter, more delicate touch—like filleting a trout, whittling a marshmallow stick, or slicing food. This knife should be sturdy and well made, but remember that no hinged blade is suited to abuses like chopping and prying; in this instance a long-lived razor-keen edge has more value than brute strength. Like your sheath knife, a working folder should have a handle that won't slip in your hand when wet or coated with fish slime, and like a sheath knife, you should be able to deploy it using just one hand.

The folding belt knives I like best for backpacking include the big Buck Crosslock ($60), which opens with just a flick of the thumb. Gerber's E-Z Out ($40) is a well-crafted ambidextrous one-hander with an integral belt clip instead of a holster, but I lost my sample somewhere in the Upper Peninsula—don't count on any belt clip to hold in rugged terrain. The Spec Plus folding jump knife from Ontario Knife ($35) is a simple masterpiece of function and utility; its 4⅛-inch epoxy-coated blade snaps open with a flick of the wrist and has all the fine qualities of 1095 spring steel. I like the Tomcat from SOG Specialty Knives ($80), but while this 3½-inch-blade brute is built to be unbreakable, the Kraton (rubber) scales in my sample's handle pulled loose and had to be reglued, it's not a one-hander, and I wasn't impressed by its edge retention.

In addition to a sheath folder I always carry a quality pocketknife for everyday chores like cutting rope, cutting cardboard, and stripping an occasional wire—jobs you wouldn't want to dull your sheath folder on. The almost elegant bone-handled Case XX Copperlock ($40), with its locking 3-inch blade, looks as good filleting a salmon as it does cutting carpet, and it does both very well. I also like Case's Sodbuster Jr. ($30), which isn't a lockback

The Spec Plus folding jump knife (model SPF52).
Courtesy Ontario Knife Co.

The SP-8 survival machete. *Courtesy Ontario Knife Co.*

but has a wide, deep-bellied blade that skins small game and cleans a horse's hooves with equal utility. My favorite pocketknife overall is the classic three-blade Stockman's Knife, which always seems to have at least one sharp blade and retails for about $20 from Buck, Schrade, Case, and Queen Cutlery.

Next are the camp knives—large, strong blades that can be used for the chopping, hacking, and digging jobs a typical survival knife hasn't the length or weight to do well. Day hikers, cross-country skiers, and folks who plan to be in the woods for less than a day have little need for such large blades, but I strongly recommend that any backpacker have a functional camp knife lashed to his pack.

I've searched for the perfect camp knife since boyhood, even to the point of packing a handmade job (ground from M1 Abrahms battle tank armor) for several years. The venerable GI jungle machete, combat-proven against bamboo, lianas, and the other guy, has repeatedly shown a nasty tendency to snap in two roughly 6 inches from its handle when pitted against woods like maple, oak, and birch. Inexpensive (about $10) look-alikes with hollow plastic handles that vibrate painfully against the palm while you're chopping don't break, but their mild-steel blades are soft and will nick or bend with rough use.

The best heavy-duty camp knife I've found yet, and the one you'll find strapped to the side of my own backpack until something better comes along, is the SP-8 from the Ontario Knife Company ($50). A full ¼ inch thick, its squared-front 10-inch blade of epoxy-coated 1095 spring steel sports a row of unique double saw teeth along its spine. Ontario's distinctive Spec Plus molded-Kraton handle provides a positive grip when wet or used with gloves, and the blade's sharpened, flat fore-end works

Kukri camp knife (model 35LTC). *Courtesy Cold Steel, Inc.*

well for chiseling, digging, or prying tasks. Heavy weight, short length, and a powerful chopping stroke combined with unmatched brute strength make the SP-8 a first-rate backpacking machete. The big knife is sold with a handsome Cordura-and-leather sheath that can be worn on a belt or (my preference) tied onto a wilderness-bound backpack.

My second choice in camp knives is the Kukri from Cold Steel ($45). This large knife, with its distinctively curved 12-inch epoxy-coated blade, is best known as the constant companion of Gurkha tribesmen in India and Burma. The kukri served with distinction in World War II; indeed, it's still the issue knife of Her Majesty's Gurkha Regiment. The Cold Steel version, made from that company's proprietary Carbon V alloy, is the finest and sharpest kukri ever made, right out of the box, and it holds its edge phenomenally well against hard woods. The no-slip Kraton handle is comfortable while chopping, and the kukri's trademark point-heavy design results in a powerful stroke that belies the knife's weight and size.

A favorite with small-framed ladies, youngsters, and novices who don't feel quite safe from themselves while wielding a large blade is the Bolo Knife from Ontario Knife ($35). Like the kukri, bolo knives have bellied-out blades that are wider at the point than at the handle, but in this instance the blade and handle are in line with each other instead of being curved. With the same length, Kraton handle, and powder-coated blade as the SP-8, the Bolo's blade is half as thick and less tiring to smaller arms.

Portable Water Filters

Whenever I happen across a piece of romantic literature that refers to pristine lakes and streams so pure a buckskin-clad frontiersman could drink from them with impunity, I have to smile. This planet's waters have never been safe for humans or other animals to drink untreated. Mild to sometimes fatal illnesses from amoebic, bacterial, viral, and chemical sources have always plagued mankind, and "civilization" has done little to make natural waters safe to bathe in, let alone drink.

Making water safe enough

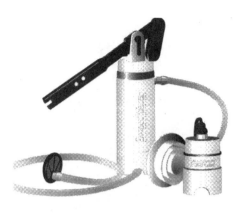

The SweetWater Guardian+Plus water filter. *Courtesy SweetWater.*

for consumption has never been complicated—I cover several methods in chapter 8—but today's technology makes the process simpler than ever. The best purification tool to appear since fire is the pump-type filter, which uses a plunger to force chambered water under great pressure through a micron-pored filter that removes 99.9999 percent of all waterborne organisms. Viruses tiny enough to get through the filter are destroyed by passing through an iodized final stage, and then to the outlet port, from which you can fill your canteen with safe drinking water. Having thoroughly field-tested the 14-ounce SweetWater Guardian+Plus ($70) and the 11-ounce Voyageur from Pur (also $70; see the source list on pages 48–52), I now wonder how I ever got along without a water purifier, and today I wouldn't think of backpacking without one.

The PUR Voyageur water filter. *Courtesy PUR Drinking Water Systems.*

Using the average pump-type filter is child's play: Push the unit's inlet and outlet hoses onto their respective nozzles, toss the inlet hose into raw water, and pump potable water from the outlet hose into a canteen, onto a wound that needs cleansing, or directly into your mouth. Prefilters on inlet hose ends keep out silt and sediment

Purifying water in black fly season with the PUR Voyageur.

that might clog filters prematurely, and flow rates average roughly 1 liter per minute, lessening as filters become more clogged from use. Filter cartridges for the Voyageur will purify 100 gallons of water, 200 gallons for the Guardian+Plus; replacement cartridges cost $40 and $20, respectively. Considering the value a microfilter could have both on the trail and at home during a flood or some other disaster that makes potable water scarce, it wouldn't be a bad idea to keep one in the house and another in the backpack. One concern I had initially was that subfreezing temperatures might cause the filters to freeze solid after use, but neither of my test samples functioned any differently in winter than in summer.

I do, however, recommend that you isolate the intake hose and prefilter in a plastic bag before placing them back into the unit's stuff sack. Just stuffing the entire unit back into its sack after use creates the potential for parasite-infested water to reach and contaminate the output hose. Kind of defeats the purpose, doesn't it?

Footwear

No buying decision you make could have more regrettable consequences than inadequate pairs of boots and socks. Without footwear suited to the climate and terrain you're in, you run the risk of frostbitten toes, blisters, sprained ankles, falls, and other assorted injuries. If you can baby only one part of your body, let it be your feet, because without them you're stranded.

Socks

"Dry socks are far more important than clean underwear." This wilderness axiom actually understates the importance a good pair of socks can have for any hiker's comfort level in any season. Thick, well-cushioned socks can eliminate the sore spots and rubbing that occur on long hikes, pad the hard spots in new boots, and add tremendously to the comfort and warmth of any outdoor footwear.

For several years now hikers of all disciplines have recognized the value of a two-sock system consisting of a lightweight, slippery liner under a thick—usually wool—oversock. The trend began with hikers wearing light acrylic dress socks under wool hiking socks; today sock makers have taken that basic good idea to a level of technology all their own. These are definitely not the same coarse woolies I wore while hunting and trapping in my youth.

Of all the socks I've walked on for days at a time, my overall favorites in terms of price, comfort, and quality were made by Wigwam Mills, Inc., of Sheboygan, Wisconsin. Best known as a maker of rugged wool outer socks, Wigwam also makes the best liner socks I've tried. Its Ultimax liner ($8 a pair) is an all-synthetic blend of slippery, moisture-repellent fibers woven into a thin but very dense fabric that effectively wicks perspiration away from the skin while protecting against blisters. For light day hiking, I really like the luxuriously soft merino wool liners ($7); I consider them an ideal inner sock for beginners whose feet haven't yet toughened to the demands of rugged boots on rough terrain.

Wigwam's heavyweight woolen outer socks also get high praise from me in the areas of warmth, comfort, and durability. The cushy merino wool CoolMax hiker ($14) is my preference for long walks in hot weather when the terrain demands heavyweight boots, but the Ultimax is a very good all-around hiker and retails for $12. At the other end of the spectrum are the Fairbanks, 40 Below, and Polar socks, which all proved to be the warmest thermal socks I've worn when used with a good liner. These retail for about $12 at most outfitters.

A recent entry into the hiking and backpacking sock arena is the WrightSock, made by Wrightenberry Mills of Graham, North Carolina. For many years a leader in the high-end running and athletic sock markets, Wrightenberry has a lot of real-world savvy to offer, and it

Wigwam Ultimax Rugged Outdoor socks.
Courtesy Wigwam Mills Inc.

shows in the company's first attempts at making thoroughbred hiking boot socks. Its Double Layer socks incorporate a liner of CoolMax or Thermastat material interwoven with MicroSafe AM, an antibacterial, antifungal fabric. The liner is mated to a heavy wool-blend outer shell to form a unit that makes keeping track of socks and liners half as tough, eliminates chafing, and provides outstanding comfort. Since the liners and socks come already mated, these were by themselves the warmest socks I've tried, though slightly less warm and cushiony than conventional woolen outer socks with separate liners. The one problem I encountered with my samples was that laundering caused the liner to slide and twist inside the outer sock, which made getting both layers fitted to the foot a tedious matter. The retail price for these handy combination socks is about $18.

The most radical sock I've evaluated is the Porelle Drys model from Porvair Fabrics, Ltd., of Northampton, England. With a price tag of $35 per pair, Porelle Drys had me expecting something special, and I must admit that they're in a class by themselves. Most notable is the fact that these two-layer socks are 100 percent waterproof, with a patented polyurethane membrane between inner and outer layers that truly keeps water out while at the same time keeping feet dry by wicking away perspiration.

No other sock performs both these functions, which means that Porelle Drys have uses heretofore unheard of from conventional hiking hosiery. I really like wearing them when I sleep, especially if the weather is wet or snowy, because they prevent wet feet during those inevitable middle-of-the-night runs to the camp pee tree. Also very cool is the way they turn any pair of hikers into boots suitable for walking across creeks, through marshes—virtually any situation in which conventional boots and socks will result in feet that squish unpleasantly with every step. Drys aren't the warmest socks I've tried, although they do qualify as thermal, but anyone who's felt the numbing rush of icy springwater seeping through boots and socks to bare skin can appreciate the warm barrier of waterproof insulation they provide. Drys are also unique in being the only socks made in precise shoe sizes: If you wear a size 9½ shoe, you'll wear a size 9½ Porelle Dry.

Hiking Boots

While good socks are important, they're really just padding under the armor of a boot. Hiking boots protect our fragile human feet from natural and man-made hazards that would otherwise injure them, they support our ankles and keep them from twisting on uneven ground, and provide us solid traction on most slippery surfaces. Tennis shoes, loafers, and other types of "walking" shoes are not adequate when your destination is on the other side of flooded streams, deadfall swamp, or razor-edge rock. Toss a heavy backpack into the equation and good hiking boots become mandatory.

The cost of a quality hiking boot can reach $300 or better, and while I'm going to recommend several of what I consider the finest outdoor boots ever made, beginners faced with purchasing an entire backpacking outfit can get by for under $100. Light hikers, by definition, don't provide the stiff ankle support or protection needed for the really rough stuff. Still, their light weight and flexibility give them tennis-shoe-like comfort on the trail, but with the aggressive lug-style traction needed to negotiate muddy slopes and rain-slick wood.

My first choice in the light hiker category is the Sierra Trilogy from Hi-Tec (see the source list on page 49), an ankle-high light hiker whose price belies the quality and innovation incorporated into its design. Suede leather uppers guarantee that the shoes—and your feet—will be soaked after just a short walk in dewy grass, and the first step I'd recommend is a waterproofing treatment with NikWax suede formula. Beyond this relatively minor problem, the Sierra Trilogy is a very good light hiker, with innovations like a ComforTongue that better distributes lace tension over the instep to prevent sore spots in that tender area. A hard, springy plastic insert called a Tendon/Shank Suspension Midsole effectively cushions the heel from shock, while providing

The Rock-Hi boot has a soft sole that makes little noise. *Courtesy Sorel.*

a springy arch support that doesn't break down over time. The Sierra Trilogy retails for about $100.

My second choice in the low-price light hiker category is the new Rock-Hi from Sorel, priced at about $110. The first thing you notice about these is their extremely light weight and softness underfoot—great for wildlife photographers who need a quiet, soft-soled boot that makes as little noise as possible. Construction of the Rock-Hi consists of a unique design of overlapping, double-stitched, treated-leather sections that are actually more rugged and supportive than a one-piece leather upper of equal thickness. The boot isn't waterproof, but its treated leather does repel dew and light rain. My one complaint, which has yet to manifest itself as a problem, is that the nylon strap-type lacing loops that serve as eyelets on Rock-Hi models will eventually snag on brush, become frayed, and tear through.

GENERAL FEATURES

1. Two-piece tongue
2. Propex panel
3. Semirigid inner side support
4. Nubuck uppers
5. Rubber outsole
6. Polyurethane midsole
7. STONG insole
8. P. E. footbed
9. Rigid support with joint
10. Toecap
11. TPU ankle support
12. Protective rubber ankle padding
13. Hook speed lacing
14. Antitendinitis collar

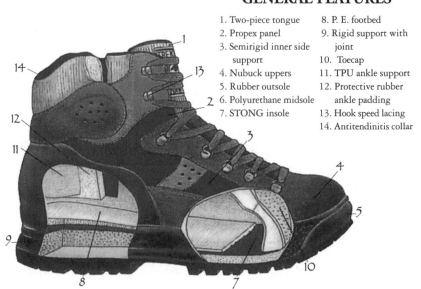

Typical light hiking boot. *Courtesy Kaufman Footwear.*

The next step up the line are the thoroughbred backpacking boots, boots designed and constructed to take on the toughest terrain comfortably and safely while their wearer is carrying a heavy pack. These boots are not cheap—most are priced at around $200—but when the terrain demands maximum ankle and arch support, unfailing traction, and protection for the feet, a backpacking boot is your best answer.

Number one among the backpacking boots I've field-tested is the Merrell M2 Superlight from Karhu USA. This is a very rugged, exceptionally comfortable boot on any terrain, and with a price tag of $150, the M2 is also a best buy in the category of serious outdoor footwear. A uniquely contoured tread made from rows of multidirectional lugs that extend clear to the toecap provides good traction in any direction, and virtually eliminates that annoying toe slip that occurs on sand, snow, and mud. A heavily padded two-layer tongue consisting of a conventional padded tongue under a heavy leather outer one allows the laces to be pulled extra tight for increased ankle support and a snug custom fit between boot and foot. Heavy double-thick rubber toecaps permit the abuse of kicking footholds into snow-covered slopes without hurting either shoes or toes. The M2 isn't waterproof and doesn't claim to be, but it will keep your feet dry for about 30 minutes of walking through wet grass in a hard rain.

My next favorite backpacking boot is the Swiss-made Mountain Trekker from Raichle. It would probably be my overall favorite except for its rather steep $300 price tag, which I must admit is justified by the product. Nearly equal to the M2 in terms of comfort, traction, and quality, the Mountain Trekker is a Rolls-Royce among backpacking boots. Six-inch top-grain leather uppers provide outstanding ankle support, and laces extend to the toes to allow a better overall fit, but the Mountain Trekker's most impressive feature is its inner lining, which is made entirely of leather. This helps explain the price tag, but practical reasons for such a seemingly lavish feature include a marked resistance to absorbing foot odors, unheard-of durability, and a liner that can be treated with any leather wax.

Next comes Red Wing's Native, a new addition to the company's respected Irish Setter line. Midpriced at $200, this is a moderate-weather boot with 400 grams of Thinsulate insulation under Gore-Tex ankle panels that help keep feet warm and dry. Shallow lug soles offer

The Irish Setter Native sports boot.
Courtesy RedWing Shoe Co.

good traction on trails and upland terrain, while a one-piece 9-inch leather upper and tongue shrugs off moisture and provides solid ankle support. The only flaws I could find in my sample consisted of a single small bunch of sewn liner material near the inside seams of each boot, both in different locations but obtrusive enough to cause initial sore spots until they were flattened through wear. Aside from this, the Native was nearly perfect in terms of comfort and wearability, though a little too warm for hot weather.

If your travels are going to include terrain where maximum strength, traction, and foot protection are required, you might opt for a heavy backpacking boot with crampon (strap-on ice claws) grooves in heel and toe. Vasque, the Italian division of Red Wing, has made a name for itself since 1965 by offering brutally strong boots, many of which are specially engineered to accommodate the lighter bone structure of a lady's foot. My wife thoroughly field-tested Vasque's Alpine model in winter and summer, and she says it's the finest outdoor boot she's worn, needing almost no break-in period. The all-leather Alpine is waterproof right to its tops, provides enough support to make twisted ankles a near impossibility, and offers a very aggressive self-cleaning lug sole to compensate for the weight difference between the sexes. Very stiff soles give the boots stability on loose ground, and I'm more than a little impressed by the Alpine's quality and rugged construction. The ladies' Alpine retails for $250 (about the same for the men's version), but most folks can count on a lifetime of wear from their investment.

La Sportiva is best known as a maker of expedition-quality mountain boots that can tackle any peak on earth, and this obsession with unfailing ruggedness and durability is obvious in the company's Pacific Crest heavy backpacking boot ($230). In fact this was the least-comfortable boot I tested, but it was also indisputably the toughest, shrugging off abuses like broken rock without so much as a scar while providing more ankle support than most hikers need. Also equipped with crampon grooves for ice climbing, the Pacific Crest feels like you have bulldozers on your feet. Aggressive self-cleaning lugs bite hard into icy surfaces, and ultrastiff soles feel as if you could kick toeholds into a brick wall.

Be aware, however, that this armorlike boot demands the best oversock-and-liner system available; my samples darned near gave me blisters several times before I finally broke them in (which took about 40 miles). Clumsiness is minimal for such brutelike footwear, they were surprisingly warm in snow, and the silicone-impregnated leather has never gotten wet or leaked.

Note, too, that the more ruggedly a boot is built, the more time it will take to conform to the contours of an individual foot. Absolutely never wear a new pair of boots into the wilderness, with or without a backpack, until you've walked them in to the point where no sore spots or areas of heavy rubbing exist. Ironically, this is where many cheaper, lighter boots have the advantage—they're trail-ready right out of the box.

Any dependable pair of hiking boots deserves routine maintenance to keep them that way. Even good factory waterproofing treatments are eventually worn away, and when boot leather becomes scuffed and pale, it will begin to absorb water into its unsealed pores. Leather treatments like Mink Oil, Bear Grease, and petroleum jelly were good when no alternatives were available, but today I use and freely recommend leather treatments from the NikWax Company. Unlike oils and greases that soften leather, diminishing a boot's ankle support and making it more vulnerable to outside damage, NikWax uses a hard wax kept in liquid suspension by a mild solvent. The solvent component is thin enough to penetrate deep into leather pores, taking dissolved wax with it; then it evaporates, leaving a waterproof layer of hardened wax that wears as long as many factory treatments. Wash your treated boots after every outing with warm water and leather cleaner to remove mud and other abrasives that can work their way into seams and eventually wear through a seam's stitching.

Sandals

If someone had told me 10 years ago that I'd be wearing sandals in the summer woods, I'd have thought him insane. Then I bought my first pair of new-generation sandals three years ago, and they've been included in my warm-

Modern hiking sandal. *Courtesy Teva.*

weather outfit ever since. I still wear rugged boots in rugged country, but for hiking established trails in hot weather, no footwear is more comfortable than sandals.

Modern hiking sandals are essentially hiking boots without the boot. A soft, flexible sole with aggressive traction provides nonslip traction equal to that of hiking boots, while adjustments at toe, heel, and instep prevent the foot from sliding on uneven terrain. But unlike even the most waterproof of hikers, modern sandals are made for wading through water past the knees, protecting the soles from sharp rocks while allowing the feet to dry as soon as you step back onto dry ground. I also find them preferable for wading muddy lakeshores, although I always wear socks as protection against bloodsuckers and leeches.

There are several sandals in the $20 range that meet my criteria for hiking and wading, but, again, you get what you pay for, and I've torn straps from their moorings twice on inexpensive sandals. If you want a quality sandal that will do everything I just mentioned without coming apart under heavy stress, Teva is the brand I most recommend. I've worn its Universal model with the Approach strapping system, Spider Rubber soles, and built-in shock absorbers as hard as my feet would allow, and I have no complaints. The price of this sandal is about $80.

Winter Boots

When snow covers the ground, experienced winter campers put away the hikers until spring and switch to pac-boots with (usually) removable liners, so named because they were designed for wear on hardpack snow. Insulated hiking boots are adequate for short-term outings like day-packing on snowshoes, but they can't cut it when you're outside for days at a time, especially not if you'll be spending long hours motionless in a photography or hunting blind. I've known too many people with missing toes who've proved this.

Today's pac-boot manufacturers have taken advantage of modern materials and technology to create the warmest, lightest, most comfortable winter footwear in history. With an average comfort rating (based on a normal walking pace) down to -100 degrees Fahrenheit, the warmest pac-boot models are the equals of any cold on earth. The challenge now is to make the once heavy and bulbous pac-boot as much like a hiking boot as possible, and there have been some impressive attempts by several manufacturers that came close.

Choosing a favorite was tough, but I finally had to go with the LaCrosse Winter Breaker -100. Comfort, quality, warmth, and rugged durability are givens with all the boots I present here, but what tipped the scales in LaCrosse's favor were knee-high leather uppers that provide a valuable increase in protective coverage for shins and ankles. The Winter Breaker is a heavy boot by today's standards, but not prohibitively so. The environmentally friendly bobsole tread, made useful only by aggressive lugs around the sole perimeter, doesn't impress me, but it works well enough on snow. The retail price is about $190.

With a pair weight of just 3½ pounds, the Snow Stalker from Rocky Shoes & Boots is the lightest pac-boot I've worn, despite being one of the warmest. Very thin reflective liners contribute to this light weight, as do large Cordura and Gore-Tex evaporation panels on the ankles. My samples held up very well to kicking around woods and camp, but the Cordura panels allowed a good deal of moisture to wet the liners from outside. I fixed this by sealing them completely with NikWax fabric treatment. Retail for the Snow Stalkers is $150.

Snow Stalker boots. *Courtesy Rocky Shoes & Boots.*

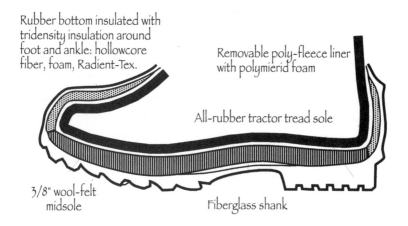

Rubber bottom insulated with tridensity insulation around foot and ankle: hollowcore fiber, foam, Radient-Tex.

Removable poly-fleece liner with polymierid foam

All-rubber tractor tread sole

3/8" wool-felt midsole

Fiberglass shank

Pac-boot construction. *Courtesy LaCrosse Footwear.*

Sorel's Alaska represents Kaufman Footwear's finest attempt yet at creating a pac-boot that can handle a day on snowpacked trails as well as a good hiker can in summer. Soft but aggressive lug soles provide good footing on nearly any surface, while air-cushioned insoles and exceptional arch support greatly diminish the relief you'll feel at taking them off after a long day of walking. Also rated to -100 degrees Fahrenheit, the Alaska is lightweight and comfortable, and has all the durability you would expect from Sorel. A pair sells for about $180.

If you prefer a more traditional winter boot, Steger Mukluks and Moccasins offers a diverse line of very nice moosehide mukluks with gum-rubber soles. If you've never worn mukluks, their nicest features are light

weight and tennis-shoe-like comfort, combined with knee-high uppers that help guard the shins and trap an extra layer of dead air. The problem, as I discovered after destroying two pairs of canvas-and-rubber air force mukluks in record time, is that many are on the flimsy side. Steger's mukluks are the exception: Every model is

The Sorel Alaska Pac-boot. *Courtesy Kaufman Footwear.*

built on a thick moosehide lower. Those made for serious outdoor activities, like running the Iditarod (really), are all moosehide from sole to knee, but there are some striking wool Indian-blanket models that I guarantee will turn heads around town or on a snowmobile safari. Steger doesn't assign temperature ratings, but I've never gotten cold toes in a pair of mukluks, and I consider them the equals of any cold if you wear good socks and change to a dry pair as needed. Stegers aren't cheap, either; the base models start at about $130, but the company does give a buyer his money's worth.

If money is a concern, you can hardly go wrong with the proven performance of a GI Mickey Mouse boot, so named because they make a wearer's feet look bulbous, like the cartoon character's. With a pair weight of 6 pounds, these are the heaviest pac-boots, made entirely of rubber and rubberized canvas. Rated to -60 degrees Fahrenheit, the Mickey Mouse boot is built like a bulldozer, but its best feature—one that I'm surprised hasn't been incorporated into commercial pac-boot designs—is a sealed liner that cannot get wet. If water enters through the tops of the boots, simply remove and dump them, wring out your socks, and put everything back on. I'm not crazy about the MM boot's tractor-tread soles, although traction is adequate, but I do like the tall heels, the good arch support, and a molded ledge on the outer heel that prevents snowshoe bindings from slipping off. Retail is about $70.

Handwear

Conventional wisdom says that the primary difference between humans and animals is our capacity for forming ideas and strategies too complex to be understood by the mental faculties of other animals. A lifetime of observation has convinced me that fingers are also a trademark of intelligence, because so many of the smartest animals have them. A grand idea means little if you lack the means to transform it from thought to reality, and since fingers are this means, it pays to keep yours in good working order in the woods.

Quality handwear isn't just for cold weather. I consider a pair of stout leather work gloves necessary in any season, and the way my gloveless companions keep borrowing them only confirms their value.

Leather is still the most rugged material available, and gloves made from it are ideal for protecting the hands while working with a campfire, chopping wood, or wending your way through a brier patch. Leather gloves from the Wells-Lamont company have always served me well and are priced at an affordable $10 to $14. Both insulated and uninsulated shells are available, but my preference is a single pair of uninsulated shells large enough to accommodate GI wool glove liners when the weather turns cold. Glove liners retail for about $2 per pair at most army-navy outlets.

For most wilderness activities, leather gloves with or without liners, as temperatures demand, are the most appropriate compromise among warmth, protection, and dexterity. But in very cold weather I pocket the leather shells and don a pair of oversize insulated mittens atop the liners. Because they combine heat generated from the fingers, instead of isolating them, mittens provide unsurpassed warmth, and they can be pulled on and off easily when you encounter tasks that require fingerwork. Again, my preferred mitten material is leather, lined with synthetic fleece, sized generously to go over the cuffs of my field jacket and long enough to cover my forearm to the elbow. Ironically, the mittens that best fit all these criteria are often inexpensive imports that sell for about $10 per pair.

Backpacks

In a real sense the backpack is the glue that binds together all the components of a wilderness outfit. Inside it, contained in a single, mobile unit, is your home for the duration of a visit to the wild. Thus a good pack has to be durable, functional, and, perhaps most important, comfortable to carry when loaded.

There are three basic types of backpack: rucksacks, which are essentially large bags with shoulder straps; external-frame packs that brace loads strategically against shoulders and back; and internal-frame types that do the same, but with a more compact design. Guides, trappers, and other long-term backpackers have traditionally preferred external frames for their strength and ability to handle very heavy loads, while climbers and short-term campers like internal frames for their narrower, less bulky design.

Today these differences are becoming less distinct, because either type will carry everything a camper needs to live comfortably for a week, or to survive indefinitely. One internal-frame pack that I've used hard and liked very much is the Grand Canyon from Coleman's Peak 1 division (see the source list on page 49). With a volume of 5,500 cubic inches, this is one of the biggest packs going, capable of holding far more than my typical 60 pounds, and

Len McDougall wearing the Peak-1 Grand Canyon Backpack.

it carries a heavy load comfortably. Luxuriously padded shoulder and waist straps with lots of quick one-hand adjustments allow you to snug the pack to your body's contours until it fits like a turtle's shell. A plethora of logically placed small pockets and pouches and three large

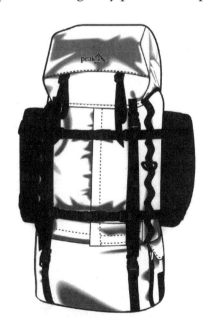

The Peak-1 Grand Canyon internal frame backpack. *Courtesy Peak 1*

isolated internal compartments prove that this pack was designed by backpackers. The Grand Canyon's useful features are too numerous to describe here, but with a price tag of $155, I rate it a best buy.

In the external-frame category consider the Super Tioga from Kelty. This pack is well known among professional outdoorsmen as one of the strongest and most functional external-frame packs this side of a large-frame military ALICE (All-purpose Lightweight Individual Carrying Equipment) pack. The

The Super Tioga backpack. *Courtesy Kelty, Inc.*

Super T boasts a number of nice features, including two zippered side pockets that provide roomy storage and fast access to often-used or emergency items. It too has well-padded shoulder and waist straps with plenty of adjustments, along with plenty of webbing loops for fastening fishing poles, a camera tripod, or other items too long or bulky to be packed inside. The Super T retails for around $190 at most outfitters.

Parents with growing youngsters might consider an adjustable-frame model that can grow with its owner, like the Scout from Jansport. Designed to fit people ranging in height from 4 feet, 6 inches, to 5 feet, 6 inches, the 3,075-cubic-inch Scout employs a locking thumbscrew-type bar that spans its frame to move the shoulder straps closer to or farther from the waist pad. This makes it an ideal first pack for

 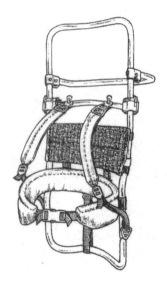

The Scout backpack has an adjustable frame which is perfect for growing children. *Courtesy Jansport*

growing youngsters and small-framed adults. Still, don't get the idea that the Scout is anything less than a serious backpack that can handle any wilderness trek. Two large main compartments and two roomy outside pockets on each side, along with a military-style top flap that separates in its center to create a place for large, thin items, make the Scout as good an external-frame pack as any, only smaller. A bonus is that you can outfit your growing backpacker for the next few years for just $50.

For daypacking and overnight excursions, I've grown fond of Eagle Creek's surprisingly rugged internal-frame Solo Journey. The Solo Journey was designed for "Euro-hiking," with shoulder and waist straps that zip inside and a carrying handle on one side that essentially turn the pack into a suitcase, but it functions well in the woods. Two load compression straps on either side allow the main compartment to be expanded, giving the pack a volume range from 3,200 cubic inches to 4,000, and interal cinch straps further allow a snug fit that eliminates annoying rattles. To me, this pack's most useful feature is it's zip-off daypack, which has its own shoulder straps and two zippered compartments with internal mesh pockets. The daypack feature lends itself well to all-day excursions away from a base camp, and I like the advantages of a single pack that can be separated into two stand-alone daypacks should the need arise. The Solo Journey retails for about $150.

The Solo Journey is perfect for daypacking or overnight trips. *Courtesy Eagle Creek, Inc.*

Sleeping Bags

For a good many years in my youth I spurned manufactured sleeping bags, opting instead to pack an equally heavy six-point wool blanket that never failed to keep me warm in rain, snow, or wind. Up to that point none of the bags I'd tried could match it pound for pound, especially not under wet, cold conditions.

Here again, things have changed greatly for the better. Key to the effectiveness of any insulation are its abilities to retain as much dead air as possible and to repel—or at least not absorb—moisture. Manufactured hollow plastic fibers like Hollofil and Quallofil do both admirably, retaining body heat almost as well wet as they do dry. Their best feature, however, is light weight; in 10 years my all-season bedroll has dropped from more than 12 pounds to just 5, including sleeping pad.

Pound for pound, goose down is still slightly more effective an insulation than synthetic fills, but despite high-quality construction—with an attendant high price—down bags aren't my first choice for backpacking. If its shell is torn, a down bag will quickly lose all of its insulation in the affected cell, while the intermeshed fibers of synthetic fills hold themselves in place until repairs can be made. Many down bags also lose loft over a period of years, with feathers clumping together and leaving insulation cells largely unfilled. My biggest objection to down, however, spawned from experience, is that the bag can become saturated, and wet feathers are about as warm as they sound.

Features to look for in any quality bag are large, self-healing coil zippers that won't fail under conditions when they can't fail, sturdy ripstop outer shells, and a generous insulation-filled draft tube that runs the full length of the bag inside the zipper to keep out cold air. Mummy-type bags are lighter, of course, because less material is used to make them, but a hooded rectangular bag is roomier and, despite claims to the contrary, no less warm than a comparably insulated mummy bag. Since most experienced backpackers employ a bag in the 20-degree Fahrenheit range for all-season use, those I'll discuss next all fall into this category.

Slumberjack's Columbia 20-degree mummy (see the source list on page 52) is one of the finest ultralight bags available at any price. Filled with 1½ pounds of Thermolite synthetic insulation, the Columbia has a total carry weight of just 3 pounds in its stuff sack (included). But it isn't light in the performance department; features like an overfilled zipper draft tube, a torso draft tube to help trap body heat, and a utility pocket to keep gloves from freezing suggest that its design came from

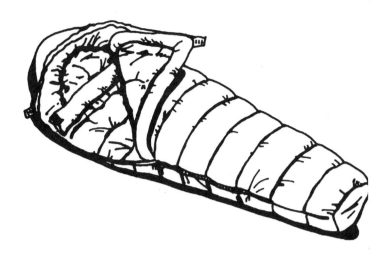

Slumberjack's Columbia sleeping bag (model EVT0286R) from the Everest Elite series.
Courtesy Slumberjack.

experience. I field-tested this bag more thoroughly than I'd intended after being stuck for two days in freezing rain with nighttime lows down to -5 degrees Fahrenheit. Even wet, the Columbia permitted a restful night's sleep with only a thin pad between it and 3 feet of hardpack. The only complaint I have is that its zipper sometimes snags on the lining. The Columbia runs about $110.

One of the nicest bags to come along in recent years is the Grey Fox from Coleman's Peak 1 division, with 40 ounces of Hollofil II synthetic insulation, a 15-degree comfort rating, and a pack weight of 6 pounds, including a really nice stuff sack. Very similar to Slumberjack's Columbia in features and overall design, the Grey Fox was also

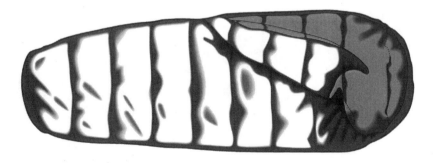

The Grey Fox synthetic filled sleeping bag from Coleman's Peak-1 division.
Courtesy Peak-1.

field-tested under very wet conditions (namely, several days of pounding rain) in temperatures that fell to 20 degrees at night. Like the Columbia, my Grey Fox's zipper exhibited an annoying tendency to snag on the fabric of its draft tube, but beyond that this bag gets a number one rating. The retail price is around $120.

If you're the kind of sleeper who likes to sprawl, or just someone who needs lots of room, a rectangular bag is the answer. My favorite in this category is Slumberjack's luxurious-feeling Hunt King, a full 36 inches across, rated to 20 degrees, and with a pack weight (no stuff sack included) of 6 pounds. An insulated drawstring hood keeps cold air from entering around your shoulders, which was always a problem in the days when sleeping bags were folded-over quilts with zippers. I've used this bag hard for three years in everything northern Michigan could throw at me, and I have no complaints. Retail for the Hunt King is $110.

If the cost of outfitting yourself for life in the wild is beginning to mount up, consider the GI Intermediate Cold mummy bag. A heavy canvas shell resists tears and moisture, its superheavy nylon zipper is backed up by a strong snap closure, and synthetic-fiber (usually Hollofil II) insulation gives the bag an actual comfort rating below 20 degrees Fahrenheit. With a good bed under me and covered by a groundsheet, I've pushed this bag to -10 degrees without losing a

Hunt King hooded rectangular sleeping bag (model SJK6001). *Courtesy Slumberjack.*

wink of sleep. The bad news is that it weighs more than 7 pounds—although this sacrifice is made less painful by a selling price of around $50 at most army-navy stores.

Sleeping bag liners are the reason most four-season backpackers can own just one sleeping bag. I've tried several over the years, including the 3-pound, scratchy wool GI models, and the one I most like is the Kala Mummy Liner from Kala Industries (see the source list on page 50). Constructed of 200-weight fleece with a heavy YKK zipper, the Kala liner weighs just 1½ pounds, doesn't absorb water, breathes well, and subtracts another 20 degrees from any bag's comfort rating. You can also use the Kala liner by itself as a summer bag in temperatures of 55 degrees or warmer. The price for a standard liner is $62, and worth it if your budget allows. If not, GI wool sleeping bag liners offer the same warmth at twice the weight, but with an average price tag of $15.

Sleeping Pads

Heat always travels to cold. That's the first law of thermodynamics, and never will that assertion be proved better than when you're sleeping on the ground. There are few places where ground temperatures are not cooler than human body temperature, and that means a camper lying directly on the ground is likely to awaken shivering in the middle of the night, even through a good sleeping bag.

Campers of old solved that dilemma by placing a bed of wrist thick branches laid side-by-side between themselves and the ground, padding the inevitable bumps with ferns, leaves, and whatever other natural mattress materials were available. It wasn't all that comfortable to sleep on, but it was better than having your body heat sucked into the ground, and in winter, a well insulated bed was simply vital to survival.

Today, technology has remedied that problem with lightweight closed-cell foam sleeping pads, made for backpacking, but also handy at the beach, for truck camping, or when relatives come to visit in force. Unlike inflatable mattresses, closed-cell foam pads remain serviceable if punctured, cut, or torn, and they never absorb water.

My personal favorite sleeping pad is the R3 model from Slumberjack, largely because its 22-inch width gives me 2 more inches of rolling room than other mats. Length is 72 inches (6 feet), which is standard for most sleeping pads, and weight is a very acceptable 16 ounces. Despite a thickness of only half an inch, I've slept comfortably on the ice of a frozen lake with only a sleeping bag and my R3 pad between my body and the ground. Retail for the R3 is about $16.

If you tend to "sleep cold," and prefer as much insulation between yourself and the ground as possible, I recommend the Z-Rest and Ridge Rest Deluxe pads, both from Cascade Designs of Seattle, WA. A full 3/4-inch thick, both models are impervious to cold and downright cushy to sleep on, but the Ridge Rest rolls up for transport in conventional fashion, while the Z-Rest folds accordian-style into a compact rectangular package that takes up less space than rolling. The Ridge Rest Deluxe and Z-Rest weigh just 18 ounces and 16 ounces, respectively, and both retail for about $25.

Campers who need extra cushioning will probably find Slumber-jacks Standard Camper self-inflating mat to their liking. Filled with open-cell foam contained in a tough airtight envelope, this pad fills by opening a valve at one corner, which allows the compressed foam to expand, sucking in air as it does so. When the foam has expanded fully, simply twist the valve closed to trap the air within and go to sleep, protected from the ground by 2 inches of softness. Like Slumberjacks R3 pad, the Standard Camper is a full 22 inches wide by 72 inches long, but its 3-pound carry weight is triple that of closed-cell foam models. Retail for the Standard Camper is about $50.

Tents

Folks who carry their home on their backs demand a great deal from a tent. It has to be light enough to carry all day, durable enough to withstand strong winds and snow, completely waterproof and bugproof, able to stand up without stakes, and roomy, yet not so costly that it sprains your wallet. That's a lot to ask, but today these qualities are pretty much the standard in quality lightweight tents.

My overall favorite tent of those I've field-tested is the Starlet from Moss Tents (see the source list on page 50). Completely made in the United States, this two-person freestanding tent has a lot more brawn than its rather wimpy name implies. Moss rates this tent as

The Moss Starlet Tent is great for any season.

three season, but I've used it through some pretty tough winter weather with no complaints. Its setup is fast enough to avoid getting wet in a sudden shower, and it has many useful features designed into a package that weighs 5 pounds, 4 ounces. The price for all of this quality is a hefty $350, and worth it if your budget allows.

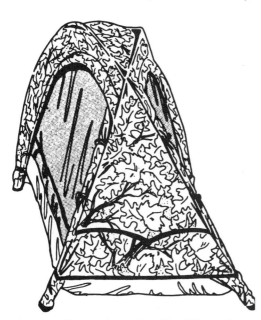

The camouflage-patterned rainfly of the Predator (model SJK7163) makes this a choice shelter for wildlife photographers and hunters alike. *Courtesy Slumberjack.*

My second favorite is the Predator from Slumberjack. The Predator is actually a large bivy shelter, rated for one person but spacious enough to accommodate a large man and his backpack in comfort. Two big doors allow access from either side and can be rolled back to spend clear nights in the open air, safe from biting insects behind

The Sola by Integral Design is perfect for the minimalist camper.

impenetrable no-see-um netting. The shelter's low, rounded profile stands up very well in driving rain and snow, and although the Predator is rated for three-season use, I've weathered more than a few winter storms inside it. This tent's rainfly is patterned in Advantage camouflage and has become a favorite with outdoor photographers and hunters, who use it as a concealable, transportable blind. One disadvantage is its weight—a hefty 7½ pounds. If camouflage isn't important to you, the Raptor model is identical to the Predator, except that it has a blue rainfly and weighs in at 6½ pounds. The price for either runs about $130.

If tight quarters concern you less than the weight of your pack, the Sola from Integral Designs is an ultralight basic shelter that has really impressed me. I'm not fond of the small door located at the front end, which forces feet-first entry, guaranteeing you'll drag some mud, water, and debris into the shelter with you. Once you're situated, however, the Sola offers plenty of room at the head for overnight necessities like flashlight, camp slippers, and chocolate-covered peanuts. Though it's not camouflaged, this bivy's low profile and dark brown color make it easy to conceal, while its very small footprint requires little more area than a sleeper's body. With a stuff-sacked carry weight of less than 3 pounds, the Sola is an ideal choice for minimalist camping. The retail price is $230.

Lighter yet at 2½ pounds is the Advanced Bivy Sack from Outdoor Research, essentially a sleeping bag oversack with a weatherproof, bugproof door at the open end, which is held open by two arced poles. The sack itself is made entirely of Gore-Tex, with waterproof taped seams. If you aren't claustrophobic, the Basic Bivy Sack is cozy, and its small footprint allows you to set up camp virtually anywhere. Be warned that this bag poses a suffocation hazard when zipped fully shut—a fact I discovered the hard way the first rainy night I slept in it. Folks who roll in their sleep might also pull the poles from their snap-down sockets, causing the doorway to collapse, but this alone doesn't pose a breathing hazard. A little duct tape around the pole ends makes them fit more tightly in their sockets. Too, I've noticed that condensation builds up in the foot portion of the bivy, and contrary to manufacturers' claims, Gore-Tex doesn't breathe well enough to stop this minor problem. The retail price for this otherwise very good minimalist four-season shelter is $229.

Whichever tent you choose, proper care is essential. Never wash your tent in any type of washing machine or I guarantee it will leak. It's okay to wipe the fabric down with a damp cloth, but use no detergents. Never snap shock-corded pole ends together, especially not with fiberglass poles; this deforms the ends and may cause poles to splinter. Dry your tent thoroughly after every use to prevent mildew (even nylon will rot), and re-treat the fabric with a quality weatherproofing spray, like TX Direct from NikWax.

Binoculars

Sharp long-distance eyesight is the only sensory advantage *Homo sapiens* has over his "lesser" cousins, most of which have little need to see far in their forest homes. Like all species designed for killing, humans have both eyeballs facing forward (prey animals that need as wide a field of view as possible have one eye on each side of the head). This restricts our field of view but provides binocular vision, an adaptation that allows the brain to constantly compare images received through each eye to accurately gauge distance and depth. Bobcats and wolves seeking to make a deadly lunge at prey need both eyes working in unison, sending a constant stream of visual comparisons that tell the body how far to leap and when to strike. The same applies to a human archer making judgments about where his arrow will impact.

Take this visual advantage and enhance it 7, 8, or 10 times, and you can see how advantageous it is to have a good binocular if you want to observe wildlife. My favorite of those I've used is the American-made Golden Ring 10x28 rubber-armored mini bino from Leupold. This is a roof-prism binocular, with straight barrels that give it a more streamlined configuration than conventional porro-prism binos, whose ocular (eyepiece) lenses are offset from the objective lenses. A length of 5½ inches allows the GR 10x28 to fit easily into a button-down breast pocket, while independent focus knobs on each barrel make getting them both in agreement fast and precise. Ten times magnification is as much as a person can hold steady in his hands, but the optics in this bino are as sharp and clear as any I've used. With a price tag of $640, they'd better be.

If you need both a binocular and a spotting scope, the variable-power 8-20x28 UCF model from Pentax (see the source list on page 51) can fulfill both those needs quite well. This is a porro-prism model, slightly bulkier than I like to carry but still small enough to wear under a jacket. Any inconvenience it may have as a binocular, however, is more than offset when you screw the Pentax onto any conventional camera tripod and turn it up to 20X for use as a spotting scope. Twenty power is far too much for most folks to hold steadily in the hands, but it's just right for stationary observation posts in the field or on the shooting range. Moreover, spotting scopes by definition don't provide binocular vision, which comes in handy for estimating how far one object is beyond another. The retail price of the 8-20x28 UCF is $330.

If you can have just one bino for everything, though, it's hard to beat a good mini binocular. These pocket-size binos have been dropping

Binoculars, from left to right: Pentax 8-20x28 UCF, Vivitar 8x21, Tasco 8x21, Leupold 10x28 Goldring.

in price, and today you can pick up quality models at most sporting goods and department stores for about $40. Two models I've used and can recommend are the Tasco 8x21 and the Simmons 8x28, both rubber armored, and both well worth the selling price.

Communications

Radio communications have been an important part of human life since Italian physicist Guglielmo Marconi changed it forever with the first transatlantic wireless transmission in 1901. He couldn't have foreseen how that first clacking of a telegraph key would so quickly lead to the bathing of the entire planet with radio, microwave, and laser transmissions.

Backpack radio receivers have been an important component of my wilderness kit since the first 9-volt, 7-transistor AM models made them portable and reliable enough to carry afield. Having advance warning of impending storm fronts via local news broadcasts has saved me considerable aggravation more than once, and today no campsite is so remote that it isn't linked to the outside world by radio broadcasts—providing, of course, that you have an operational receiver with which to hear them.

I hate to admit it, but the made-in-China AM-FM receivers that run on two AA batteries and retail for $5 at Wal-Mart are good back-pack radios for folks on a budget. Reception is surprisingly good, with good selectivity (the ability to fine-tune radio broadcasts), and the average unit will deliver about 25 hours of clear play on a fresh pair of alkalines.

But these won't be good enough if a national disaster occurs (viruses, earthquakes, nuclear terrorism . . . who knows?) that prompts a news blackout in North America. In such a situation, overseas short-wave broadcasts might prove a camper's best source of info about current events here. For this you'll need a rugged, reliable receiver capable of picking up more frequency bands than just AM and FM. Barring all of this, international shortwave is just fun to listen to.

Notable by their absence in this section are many otherwise fine weather band receivers. At first blush these might seem an ideal way to keep up on changing weather conditions at camp, but retailers who hawk

The Grundig Traveller II Digital AM/FM/shortwave receiver. *Courtesy Lextronics, Inc.*

weather band receivers as backpacking radios have obviously never backpacked. Put simply, these broadcasts were designed to reach boats and aircraft that have little but open space between them and the transmitter tower; the signals just aren't strong enough to reach the deep woods. If you want a weather report in the boondocks, AM and FM are your best bets.

My favorite backpack radio so far is the Grundig Traveller II Digital ($120; see the source list on page 49), a serious yet pocket-size receiver that tunes in AM, FM, and 14 of the 50 meter-bands allocated to international shortwave. Power is supplied by three AA batteries or a 4.5-volt AC converter, and I've been very pleased with the 50-plus hours of life I've gotten from a fresh set of alkalines. Tuning is digital, with an LCD display, onboard alarm clock, dial light, and lock switch that disables all controls so the unit doesn't change stations if bumped or, worse, turn on inside your pack. A padded vinyl carrying case is included.

My second favorite backpack radio is another Grundig, the Traveller II Analog model, also an AM-FM-shortwave but with a shortwave range of five meter-bands. It too runs on three AA batteries, has an onboard alarm clock, LCD display, and vinyl carrying case, and delivers about 50 hours of play on a fresh set of alkalines. Like the TR II Digital, reception is better than you get from many full-size stereo receivers. The retail price is about $100.

Transceivers

The value of a portable two-way radio has never been lost on deep-woods backpackers, but putting that basic good idea into practice has always been a problem. For many years I and my companions hauled AM citizens band walkie-talkies, but their battery life from eight AAs was a dismal four hours, their range was often limited to ½ mile by the squeals, static, and electrical noise associated with CB, and the radios were just plain bulky. Still, they often came in handy when someone—especially kids—wandered off to explore and suddenly discovered that nothing looked familiar.

The Motorola TalkAbout 14-channel receiver.

Things have gotten better since the silicon age, and today you can equip the kids with commercial-quality UHF FM transceivers that reach up to 2 miles (1 mile dependably in my field tests) for about $130 per unit. Motorola's TalkAbout transceivers use the new Family Radio Service (FRS) band, which has 14 channels of clear, static-free communications. The units deliver ½ watt of talk power for at least 30 hours (10 percent talk, 90 percent standby) on just three AA alkalines. A rugged plastic case protects the LCD display, and the short, fat antenna is nearly indestructible, but the units have a toylike appearance that belies their real utility in the wilderness. The TalkAbout is small enough to fit into a shirt pocket, and that's probably the best place to carry it: One of my field-test units was lost in thick swamp when its belt clip came loose.

Next up in power, performance, and, of course, price are walkie-talkies that use the also-new General Mobile Radio Service (GMRS) band. Motorola's 10-channel TalkAbout Distance, descended from its first sport model, the 10X, uses 2 watts of power drawn from a nickel-cadmium battery pack or six AA batteries in the included snap-in battery tray. The battery lives for these power sources are 8 hours and 20 hours, respectively, and having the option of getting a unit back onto the air with batteries scavenged from flashlights or radio receivers is a nice feature. The TalkAbout Distance retails for about $300 per unit.

The Maxon 100G, another GMRS transceiver, has four onboard channels that you can change to dozens of frequencies with a PC, patch cord, and the company's software. Its power is supplied by a rechargeable Ni-Cad power cell clipped to the back of each unit. The 750-milliamp-hour pack (standard) delivered a reliable 30 hours of use in the field, with reliable line-of-sight communications to 3 miles, 1 mile in forest, and intermittently to almost 4 miles. An optional 1,250-milliamp-hour battery pack is available. Battery packs deliver 7.5 volts DC, and the units can be recharged from a vehicle's electrical system. AC wall chargers are included as well. The retail price for the Maxon 100G averages about $250 per unit.

Whichever radio you might select, be warned that none is impervious to water, and all of them will go silent if immersed. The damage is temporary, and the fix is to immediately remove the radio's power source—which will otherwise go dead quickly—and let the unit air-dry. Motorola's FRS TalkAbout has a waterproof bag accessory, but it proved so clumsy that no one would use it. If you're likely to be wading deep water, keep the radio clipped or carried high or, better yet, zipped into a plastic bag inside your day or fanny pack. I've also learned the hard way to remove my walkie-talkie's power source when it's not in in use, because the rigors of brush-busting can cause these units to turn on unnoticed (despite an audible beep from the Maxon), silently draining their batteries.

Flashlights

A portable source of light can literally save your life in the wilderness. With a bright beam you can signal passing planes at night, find your way through leg-breaker timber country without a moon, and generally keep going. Without light, anyone of any experience level is best advised to stay put until morning—it wasn't superstition that kept the Native American braves of old from fighting at night, but common sense born of much experience. There's nothing to be gained from adding a perhaps serious injury (a branch in the eyeball is very common) to a situation that may already be worrisome.

Fortunately, flashlights today are light-years better than the heavy, fragile, and patently unreliable D-cell jobs I used as a kid. I'll be accused of blatant commercialism here, but I've field-tested virtually every flashlight made, and the only brand I'll put my name behind at this point is Mag-Lite, from the Mag Instrument Company (see the source list on page 50). The two-AA-cell Mini-Mag has been a permanent part of my daily attire, even when I'm forced to wear Dockers slacks and a pastel tie, for more than a decade. Durability, reliability, outstanding brightness and battery life, a focusable beam, and a spare bulb in the tailcap (standard on all models) all work to eliminate any reasons I might have for not having a flashlight anywhere I go.

The Mini-Mag, which retails for about $14 with belt holster, is my workhorse because I always have it, and because depleted batteries from it still provide sufficient power to operate appliances that have lower current needs, like my radio receiver, for several hours. The light's only real failure is that its twist-on head turns too easily when the light is in its sheath. If this happens in the daytime, your Mini-Mag might stay turned on unnoticed until its batteries expire. The company won't recommend this, but I've fixed the problem a few times by applying a thin layer of beeswax pressed into the nylon threads where the head-lens assembly screws over the bulb. Barring this, a small piece of paper or plastic slipped between the contact spring in the tailcap and the batteries will prevent the light from turning on at all until the insulating material is removed.

I also have a single-AAA-cell Mag Solitaire ($10) tied to each of my survival knives by a 3-foot cord and tucked into the knives' sheath pouches. Like all Mag-Lites, it has a beam that focuses from spot to flood, aircraft-aluminum construction, and enough dependability to get you through the woods at night.

The three-D-cell Mag-Lite ($20) is a bit heavy for most backpacking excursions, but I usually tie it onto the equipment saucer (the same thing kids use for snow sliding) I tow behind me when packing into remote country on snowshoes. The big Mag's brilliant, focusable beam slices through the darkness, making it a handy tool for fishing, frogging, laying across a stump to light a tire you're changing, or sending flash signals that can be seen from several miles away at night. Still, I generally only carry it in my 4x4.

The only genuine trouble I've ever had with Mag-Lites (aside from breaking the switch in my three-D-cell when I used it to hammer tent stakes into frozen earth) is a tendency for all of them to suddenly die in subfreezing temperatures. As near as I've determined, the problem lies in a buildup of frost between switch contacts that eventually breaks the circuit. A small moisture-absorbing silica gel packet pressed in the bottom of D-cell models, under the tailcap spring, eliminates moisture inside the watertight body. With any model, holding the flashlight close to your body, under your coat, will warm it enough to operate for at least a few more minutes.

Snowshoes

For many winters I traversed the North Woods on a pair of hand-me-down bearpaw snowshoes, originally made for the military by C. A. Lund of Prescott, Wisconsin, and stamped with the year 1945 in their ash frames. I wore them while running a trapline through my teenage years, for midwinter squirrel hunting, and on countless backpacking trips into places inaccessible by any means except snowshoes. In recent years snowmobiles have become my noisy, smelly companions nearly everyplace their tracks can go, but mostly I've been alone, a quiet, plodding anachronism of simpler times when life moved slower and folks had time to count their blessings.

Then a couple of years ago I started seeing snowshoe tracks that weren't mine in some of my favorite places, and my heart always beat a little faster in hopeful anticipation. When I finally did meet a pair of young ladies on snowshoes in thick pine forest, I nearly fell off my bearpaws in surprise.

Since then encounters with fellow snowshoers have become more frequent, and personally I like the company. Most people I meet are short-term hikers who take up snowshoeing as a means of getting outside for fresh air and exercise, often to combat those extra pounds that creep onto the waist during the holidays. Whatever reason they have for being there, I'm always glad for the chance to talk to someone who doesn't have to shut off an engine to hear me.

The increasing popularity of snowshoeing as a pastime and a sport has much to do with the design of modern snowshoes. First attempts by snowshoe makers to supplant the venerable wood-and-leather designs with lightweight aluminum frames and space-age materials were mostly unimpressive, although some real improvements were made in binding design right away. Snowshoe racing and day hiking began to emerge as popular pastimes, but initially there was no real effort to address the needs of folks who break trail through deep snow, haul home on their backs, and stay out long enough to make quality pac-boots a necessity.

That's not true today. In response to the growing number of outdoor lovers who've discovered the freedom and practicality of snowshoeing, manufacturers have diversified their lines to include every discipline. I've field-tested several new heavy-duty backpacking models from American snow-

Jacque McDougall wearing Tubbs Quest Snowshoes to get through the snow.

shoe giants Tubbs and Atlas (see the source list on page 48 & 52), and while the perfect snowshoe isn't yet available, they've given me reason to retire my old bearpaws.

Tubbs's newest shoe, a 9- by 30-inch model dubbed the Quest, is a fairly radical design that exploits modern injection-molding technology to actually form tough polyurethane decking around a tubular aluminum frame. Molded-in serrations on the bottoms complement large, aggressive stainless-steel toe and heel claws to provide extra stability and traction when you're climbing hills. Quick-release strap-and-buckle bindings make getting into or out of the shoes fast and simple, and a unique swiveling platform under the ball of the foot ensures straight tracking with impressive lateral stability.

The Quest is rated for "over 170 pounds," and company reps claim it's unbreakable—a first for backcountry snowshoers, who have always needed to worry about "bridging" a shoe across two solid points (downed trees and the like) with nothing between. I must admit that mine haven't so much as creaked, despite intentionally bridging them repeatedly under as much as 250 pounds (me plus a 60-pound pack). Their flotation is nearly equal to that of the bearpaws—the shoes sink 4 to 6 inches—but the price of the Quest's durability is a pair weight of 6 pounds, or about ½ pound per shoe heavier than most comparable models. The retail price is about

The Atlas Summit 33 Snowshoe (model 1033) provides excellent maneuverability in tight places. *Courtesy Atlas Snow-Shoe Company.*

$120, which seems reasonable for the level of performance and security they provide.

Equally impressive but lighter and easier on old guys like me is the Summit 33 from Atlas's Backcountry series. With a pair weight of 3.9 pounds, it's not as stoutly built as the Quest, but the 9- by 29-inch Summit 33 is nonetheless rated for loads of 160 to 260 pounds and had no trouble supporting a 245-pound man. Tubular aluminum frames with tough Hypalon decking provide flotation equal to that of the bearpaws, and beginners generally find them easy to manipulate in the woods. Their niftiest feature is a unique ratcheting binding system that

Snowshoes, from left to right: Tubbs Quest, Atlas 1033, Blue Atlas 1233 Summit and Len's 54-year-old Bear Paws by CA Lund.

virtually makes the snowshoe an integral part of your boot and provides excellent maneuverability in tight places. Another thoughtful feature of all Atlas shoes is their heavyweight nylon carrying case, which allows you to sling them over your shoulder on hardpack trails where wearing them is awkward and unnecessary. The Summit retails for about $230.

Snowshoeing Tips

Technical innovations aside, most beginners are probably attracted to snowshoeing because anyone can master the sport in just a few minutes. Unlike cross-country skiing or learning to drive a snowmobile, first-timers can set out on a trek as soon as their bindings are tight. You don't need instructions or practice; you just need a pair of snowshoes and the legs to use them.

That said, there are a few pointers that beginners might find handy. The first is to step high. Raise each foot high and bend your knee when stepping forward to ensure that the snowshoe toes clear their own imprint and any obstacles that might be hidden just beneath the surface. Shoes should swivel downward freely at their tails each time you raise a foot, which helps them track straight, and there should be plenty of clearance between your boot toes and the shoe decking. Make certain before you set out that the shoes and bindings you have are compatible with your boots, because some hiking bindings are too small for pac-boots and vice versa.

A common mistake among first-timers is trying to stride with the snowshoes, as though walking down a sidewalk in loafers. Modern designs are more forgiving of this than traditional shoes, but short steps remain the order of the day, especially when you're breaking trail through deep powder. A good rule of thumb is to consciously take half steps, bringing your rearward shoe forward until your advancing foot is even with the toe of the opposite snowshoe. Short steps are less tiring, and they make for better shoe maneuverability in thick brush.

Steep hills have always been a problem with traditional snow-shoes, and often it was simply easier to remove them and struggle uphill through deep snow. This too has changed; all the new backcountry shoes I've seen are equipped with very aggressive stainless-steel toe and heel cleats that make molehills out of mountains. The wisdom is to never tackle a steep grade head-on from either direction, but to ascend or descend at a 45-degree angle to its face, always mindful of drifted overhangs and other potential cave-in hazards. Dig your toes in when climbing, dig your heels in when descending, and pack each step firmly underfoot before exerting weight on it.

Having said this, I'll now admit to fully pushing the new backcountry shoes to their gravity-defying limits, climbing grades I would have carried the bearpaws up, and leaping with foolish abandon down steep hillsides. I don't recommend doing the latter. Still, hills aren't nearly the trouble they used to be.

Despite the abuse I heaped onto my test samples, try not to bridge your shoes across two solid points, especially while carrying any type of heavy pack. Bridging is hard on frames and decking, and breaking one snowshoe in waist-deep snow a mile out is a serious problem indeed.

Directory of Outdoor Equipment Sources

ATLAS SNOW-SHOE COMPANY
1830 Harrison Street
San Francisco, CA 94103
Telephone: (415) 703-0414
Fax: (415) 252-0354
Products: Lightweight backcountry
    snowshoes.

ATSKO/SNO-SEAL
2530 Russell SE
Orangeburg, SC 19115
Telephone: (803) 531-1820
Products: Scent killer, Sport Wash
    UV killer, Sno-Seal boot wax.

BAUSCH & LOMB SPORTS OPTICS
9200 Cody
Overland Park, KS 66214
Telephone: (800) 423-3537
Products: Binoculars, spotting
    scopes, rifle scopes.

BRIGADE QUARTERMASTERS
1025 Cobb International Boulevard
Kennesaw, GA 30144-4300
Telephone: (800) 338-4327
Products: Military and civilian
    outdoor equipment.

BRUNTON USA
620 East Monroe
Riverton, WY 82501-4997
Telephone: (307) 856-6559
Fax: (307) 856-1840
Products: Compasses, Lakota knives,
    binoculars.

BUCK KNIVES
1900 Weld Boulevard
P.O. Box 1267
El Cajon, CA 92022
Telephone: (800) 326-2825
Products: Fixed-blade and folding
    knives.

CABELA'S
One Cabela Drive
Sidney, NE 69160
Telephone: (800) 237-4444
Fax: (800) 496-6329
Products: Outdoor equipment.

CAMPMOR, INC.
P.O. Box 700-R
Saddle River, NJ 07458-0700
Telephone: (800) 230-2154 or
    (201) 445-5000
Products: Outdoor equipment.

W. R. Case & Sons Cutlery
Owens Way
Bradford, PA 16701
Telephone: (814) 368-4123
Products: Fine folding knives.

Cold Steel, Inc.
2128-D Knoll Drive
Ventura, CA 93003
Telephone: (800) 255-4716
Products: Fine outdoor knives and
    cutting tools.

Coleman Company
250 North St. Francis
P.O. Box 1762
Wichita, KS 67201
Telephone: (800) 835-3278 or
    (316) 832-2653
Products: Peak 1 sleeping bags,
    backpacks, camp stoves.

Eagle Creek
1740 La Costa Meadow Drive
San Marcos, CA 92069-5106
Telephone: (760) 471-7600
Web site: http://www.eaglecreek.com
Products: Quality day packs and
    travel packs.

Eagle Electronics
P.O. Box 669
Catoosa, OK 74015-0669
Telephone: (800) 324-4737
Products: Expedition II Global
    Positioning System (GPS).

General Bandages, Inc.
8300 LeHigh Avenue
P.O. Box 909
Morton Grove, IL 60053
Telephone: (708) 966-8383
Fax: (708) 966-7733
Products: Safety tape and
    medical equipment.

Gerber Legendary Blades (a
division of Fiskars)
14200 SW 72nd
Portland, OR 97223
Telephone: (503) 639-6161
Products: Fine outdoor knives and
    cutting tools.

Grundig, Inc.
3520 Haven Avenue, #L
Redwood City, CA 94063
Telephone: (800) 872-2228
Products: Quality radio receivers.

Hi-Tec Sports USA, Inc.
4801 Stoddard Road
Modesto, CA 95356-0319
Telephone: (800) 521-1698 or
    (209) 545-1111
Fax: (209) 545-2543
Web site: http://www.hi-tecsports.com
Products: Midpriced hiking footwear.

Imperial Schrade Corporation
7 Schrade Court
P.O. Box 7000
Ellenville, NY 12428
Telephone: (800) 372-4723 or
    (212) 889-5700
Products: Quality fixed-blade and
    folding knives.

Integral Designs
5516 Third Street SE
Calgary, Alberta T2H 1J9, Canada
Telephone: (403) 640-1445
Fax: (403) 640-1444
E-mail: integral@agt.net
Products: Bivy shelters,
    sleeping bags.

Jansport, Inc.
10411 Airport Road
Everett, WA 98204
Telephone: (800) 426-9227 or
    (206) 353-0200
Products: Quality backpacks.

KABAR KNIVES (A DIVISION OF
AMERICAN CONSUMER PRODUCTS)
5777 Grant Avenue
Cleveland, OH 44105
Telephone: (800) 282-0130 or
(716) 372-5952
Products: Quality outdoor knives.

KALA INDUSTRIES, INC.
289 Rollins Circle
Kent, OH 44240-2159
Telephone: (330) 677-4895 or
(888) 525-2224
E-mail: kalabag@imperium.net
Products: Fleece sleeping bags and
sleeping bag liners.

KAUFMAN FOOTWEAR (SOREL)
700 Ellicott Street
Batavia, NY 14020
Telephone: (800) 667-6735
Products: Pac-boots and
lightweight hikers.

KELTY PACK, INC.
6235 Lookout Road
Boulder, CO 80301
Telephone: (303) 530-7670
Products: Backpacks, sleeping bags.

LACROSSE FOOTWEAR
1407 St. Andrew Street
P.O. Box 1328
LaCrosse, WI 54603
Telephone: (800) 323-2668 or
(608) 782-3020
Fax: (800) 654-9444
Products: Pac-boots.

LA SPORTIVA USA
3280 Pearl Street
Boulder, CO 80301
Telephone: (303) 443-8710
Fax: (303) 442-7542
E-mail: custserv@sportiva.com
Products: Heavy-duty mountain and
backpacking boots.

MAG INSTRUMENT COMPANY
1635 South Sacramento Avenue
Ontario, CA 91761
Telephone: (909) 947-1006
Products: The world's finest
flashlights.

MAJOR ARMY NAVY SURPLUS
435 West Alondro Boulevard
Gardena, CA 90248
Telephone: (800) 441-8855 or
(310) 324-8855
Fax: (310) 324-6909
Products: Military and civilian
outdoor equipment.

MAXON, ADVERTISING DEPARTMENT
10828 NW Air World Drive
Kansas City, MO 64153
Telephone: (816) 891-6320
Fax: (816) 891-8815
Products: Professional-quality
two-way radios.

MERRELL SHOES
(A DIVISION OF KARHU USA)
P.O. Box 4249
Burlington, VT 05406
Telephone: (800) 869-3348
Products: Fine hiking footwear.

MOSS TENTS
P.O. Box 577
Camden, ME 04843
Telephone: (800) 859-5322
Fax: (207) 236-9490
Products: American-made
expedition-quality tents.

MOTOROLA, LAND MOBILE
PRODUCTS SECTOR
1301 East Algonquin Road
Schaumburg, IL 60196-1078
Telephone: (847) 576-1000
Products: Professional-quality two-
way radios.

MOUNTAIN HOUSE
(FREEZE-DRIED FOODS)—SEE
OREGON FREEZE DRY, INC.

MOUNTAIN SAFETY RESEARCH
(MSR), INC.
P.O. Box 24547
Seattle, WA 98124
Telephone: (800) 877-9677
Fax: (206) 682-4184
E-mail: info@msr.e-mail.com
Web site: http://www.msrcorp.com
Products: Water filters, camp stoves, snowshoes, other outdoor gear.

NIKWAX WATERPROOFING SYSTEMS
P.O. Box 1572
Everett, WA 98202
Telephone: (206) 303-1410
Fax: (206) 303-1242
Products: Leather and fabric waterproofing treatments.

ONTARIO KNIFE COMPANY
P.O. Box 145
Franklinville, NY 14737
Telephone: (800) 222-5233 or (716) 676-5527
Fax: (716) 676-5535
Products: Fine fixed-blade and folding knives, and machetes.

OREGON FREEZE DRY, INC.
525 25th Avenue SW
P.O. Box 1048
Albany, OR 97321
Telephone: (541) 926-6001
Fax: (541) 967-6527
E-mail: mtnhouse@ofd.com
Products: Dehydrated camping foods.

OUTDOOR RESEARCH
2203 First Avenue South
Seattle, WA 98134-1424
Telephone: (800) 421-2421 or (206) 467-8197
Fax: (206) 467-0374
Web site: http://www.orgear.com
Products: Bivy shelters, sleeping bags.

PENTAX CORPORATION
35 Inverness Drive East
Englewood, CO 80112
Telephone: (303) 799-8000
Products: Cameras, lenses, binoculars, rifle scopes.

PUR DRINKING WATER SYSTEMS
9300 North 75th Avenue
Minneapolis, MN 55428
Telephone: (612) 315-5500
Fax: (612) 315-5505
Products: Backpack water purifiers and filters.

RAICHLE MOLITOR USA
Geneva Road
Brewster, NY 10509
Telephone: (914) 279-5121
Products: Top-quality hiking and mountain boots.

RED WING SHOES
Riverfront Centre
314 Main Street
Red Wing, MN 55066
Telephone: (612) 388-8211
Fax: (612) 388-7415
Products: Fine outdoor and hunting footwear.

REI OUTDOOR EQUIPMENT
P.O. Box 1938
Sumner, WA 98390
Telephone: (206) 395-3780 or (800) 426-4840
Products: Outdoor equipment.

ROCKY SHOES & BOOTS, INC.
39 Canal Street
Nelsonville, OH 45764
Telephone: (800) 421-5151 or (614) 753-1951
Fax: (614) 753-4024
Products: Lightweight pac-boots, hiking and hunting footwear.

SIMMONS OUTDOOR CORPORATION
2120 Killearney Way
Tallahassee, FL 32308
Telephone: (904) 878-5100
Products: Binoculars, rifle scopes.

SLUMBERJACK
P.O. Box 7048A
St. Louis, MO 63177
Telephone: (800) 233-6283
Products: Bivy shelters, sleeping
bags, sleeping pads.

SOG SPECIALTY KNIVES
P.O. Box 1024
Edmonds, WA 98020
Telephone: (206) 771-6230
Products: Fixed-blade and
folding knives.

STEGER MUKLUKS
(ALSO STEGER MOCCASINS)
100 Miners Drive
Ely, MN 55731
Telephone: (800) 685-5857
Products: Professional-quality
mukluks and moosehide
moccasins.

SURVIVAL, INC.
2633 Eastlake Avenue East,
Suite 103
Seattle, WA 98102
Telephone: (206) 726-9363 or
(800) 292-4707
Fax: (206) 726-0130
Products: Signal mirrors, Blast
Match and Strike Force
fire-starting tools.

SWEETWATER, INC.
2505 Trade Centre Avenue, Suite D
Longmont, CO 80501
Telephone: (800) 557-9338
Web site: http://www.sweet-
h2o.com/sweetwater
E-mail: sweet@tesser.com
Products: Backpack water purifiers.

TASCO
P.O. Box 520080
Miami, FL 33152
Telephone: (305) 591-3670
Products: Binoculars, rifle scopes.

TECNICA
19 Technology Drive
West Lebanon, NH 03784
Telephone: (603) 298-8032 or
(800) 258-3897
Fax: (603) 298-5790
Products: Quality lightweight
hiking and snowshoeing boots.

TEVA SANDALS (A DIVISION OF
DECKER'S OUTDOOR CORPORATION)
Telephone: (800) 367-8382
Web site: http://www.teva.com
Products: Canoeing, rafting, and
hiking sandals.

TUBBS SNOWSHOE COMPANY
52 River Road
Stowe, VT 05672
Telephone: (800) 882-2748 or
(802) 253-7398
Fax: (802) 253-9982
Products: Quality snowshoes.

UNITED STATES GEOLOGICAL SURVEY
Information Services
P.O. Box 25286
Denver, CO 80225
Products: Topographical maps.

VASQUE OUTDOOR FOOTWEAR
2460 S/3270 W
Salt Lake City, UT 84119
Telephone: (800) 224-4453
Products: Quality mountain and
backpacking footwear.

2

Orienteering

I've lost count of how many hikers, bikers, and anglers, along with mushroom, deer, and other hunters, I've run across who were glad to see me because they were lost. Many were on established, marked trails, and a few were even armed with compass and map, yet none knew enough about basic orienteering to get home without outside help.

Without a compass and a fundamental understanding of the service it provides, no woodsman is ever far from being entirely lost. Yet a large number of outdoor lovers continue to neglect this vital piece of equipment because they mistakenly believe that using it requires some sort of specialized training. If you're one of these, the following paragraphs may leave you kicking yourself, because virtually anyone old enough to wander away can at least be taught to follow a compass bearing—including my four-year-old granddaughter.

The Basics

The first thing to remember is that every compass, regardless of how complex it appears, actually does nothing but point to magnetic north.

Sights, lenses, mirrors, protractors, and map scales on more sophisticated compasses allow greater precision in large wilderness areas, but even the most involved calculations begin with knowing where magnetic north lies relative to your own position.

Before exploring any remote area, you should have a working knowledge of local terrain features, especially large, hard-to-miss landmarks like trails, rivers, and railroad grades. After this the first step is to take a bearing as you enter the woods—that is, to establish the direction you'll be traveling in. To find a bearing, lay the compass flat in your palm, parallel to the earth (tilting it may cause the indicator to stick), and rotate the N on the compass's graduated outer ring (bezel) until it agrees with the north—usually red or orange—half of the indicator. With these sighting tools aligned to magnetic north, south is to your rear, east to your right, and west on your left, as indicated by the compass's bezel.

Note that every compass, except for some Russian military models, is marked with 360 degrees around its circumference, just as a clock face is marked with 60 minutes. North is at both 0 and 360, just as the 12 on a clock's face marks the beginning and end of an hour or minute. East is at 90, south at 180, and west at 270 degrees. With the compass oriented to magnetic north, these graduations allow you to precisely determine the course you intend to follow (for instance, 280 degrees west by northwest).

The forward bearing, sometimes called the forward azimuth, will also provide a back bearing—the direction that leads back to your starting point. This return course is always 180 degrees away from the forward bearing. If a forward bearing lies at 105 degrees (less than 180), for example, *add* 180 degrees to it to reach a back bearing of 285 degrees. If your forward bearing lies at 310 degrees (greater than 180), *subtract* 180 degrees for a back bearing of 130 degrees.

The important thing is that a compass allows you to remain fixed on one heading in turnaround country, and despite unavoidable detours around obstacles, this will be sufficient to get you out of the woods.

Maps

To get the most out of any compass, you need a map to provide a pictorial reference for the information it gives you. Being able to positively identify landmarks with a map means you have an anchor from which to plot the next leg of your trek, and having a preview of what lies ahead can be critical to finding the easiest course through rugged country.

While even a filling station map is better than none at all, it pays to get a map designed for exploring the wilderness. Trail maps from local and state chambers of commerce, bookstores, and some libraries are a must for sorting out what is often a maze of trails and roads. Many of these are outdated and don't show recently made roads or trails, and some older trails shown might have become overgrown, but they're more than adequate for backpacking, snowmobiling, or other activities where travel will be restricted to established pathways.

For larger wilderness areas, especially in mountain country, you'll want a more detailed map that gives elevation data about peaks, ridges, swamps, and chasms that might best be skirted. In the United States that means a color topographical map from the U.S. Geological Survey (see the source list on page 52). Misshapen, concentric rings that correspond in shape to the terrain features they represent are also graduations of elevation and depression, allowing practiced hikers to navigate some terrain by simply referencing between their maps and the surrounding countryside. USGS topos are priced at $4 per map, with a shipping and handling fee of $3.50 per order, so it pays to buy several at once.

Unfortunately, most wilderness maps are too fragile for their intended use, something I learned the hard way once when I slipped off a rain-slick log while crossing a swollen river. Having your map reduced to a clump of soggy, useless paper can ruin an entire trip, because even if you aren't lost, you might not be able to reach your objective without a terrain guide.

The best way I've found to make maps trail-ready involves laminating both sides with clear adhesive-backed contact paper, which is available for about $6 a roll at most department stores. One roll will laminate several maps, depending on their sizes, and while a few wrinkles and bubbles seem inevitable, the result is a rugged map that won't rip in hard winds or get wet. The plastic surface makes it possible to mark on the map with a grease pencil or crayon, which then wipes off with a cloth, and in a pinch the map can be used to catch and funnel rainwater into a drinking vessel.

Advanced Orienteering

While a typical outdoorsman seldom needs his compass to do more than show the way to a nearby road, situations can arise that demand more advanced orienteering methods. Dodging new beaver floodings or broken bridges, making forced course changes to avoid hostile weather, or cutting cross-country to get medical help for an injured companion are all real-life possibilities.

More advanced navigation techniques require using a map and compass together, and here is where map compasses like Brunton's 8020 or Suunto's M-5DL come into their own (see chapter 1). Map compasses—including the prismatic sighting models—have see-through bases that allow you to place the instrument directly onto a map and read the two together. This makes course calculations faster and more precise than is possible with metal-body compasses.

The first step is to align both map and compass to magnetic north. To do this, place the map flat on the ground, away from metal objects that might deflect the compass indicator, and lay the compass on top of it. Orient the compass to north, as if you were taking a bearing, and rotate the map beneath it until the two are in agreement. With both instruments aligned to north, the map becomes a microcosm of the surrounding countryside; a mountain shown to your left (west) on the map will indeed be visible to your left, and the same applies to all other mapped landmarks.

It's also important to understand that there are two norths: true north, the one your map will probably be oriented to, and magnetic north, the one your compass points to. Depending on your geographic location, the difference between these two norths—called declination—in North America can range from 0 degrees in Ishpeming, Michigan, to a whopping 35 degrees along Alaska's Pacific shoreline. The 0-declination line, where compass and map agree, is a narrow strip of land extending in an irregular line from Florida's tip through Michigan's Keweenaw Peninsula. The farther east or west you travel from the 0-declination line, the greater the difference between map north and compass north, and the more important it becomes to take this difference into account when plotting a course.

Compensating for declination is easy, though. Locate your position as closely as possible using the declination chart, and if you're left (west) of the 0 line, subtract the number of degrees shown from the heading you arrived at with compass and map. If your position is right (east) of the 0 line, add the value indicated. For example, if you were in Idaho, which has a negative declination of 20 degrees, and wanted to follow a bearing of 270 degrees, the compass heading you'd follow would be at 250 degrees. Failure to compensate for declination would result in your being off course by ¾ mile after traveling just 2 miles in any direction. Magnetic declination can thus have serious consequences if you're trying to reach a remote cabin in blinding snow, fog, or torrential rain.

A surprisingly common and potentially serious mistake made by hikers crossing country where identifiable landmarks are hidden by weather or terrain is not trusting their compasses. Not long ago one of my backpacking companions, who should have known better, had to walk the 2 miles he'd missed our rendezvous by because he'd decided his compass was lying. It can be unnerving to spend hours crossing trackless

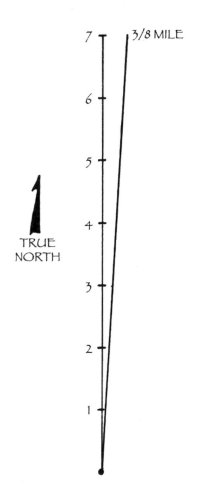

The effect of not compensating for a 3-degree declination factor over a distance of 7 miles.

wilderness with only compass and map to show you the way, but always remember that a compass cannot give a false reading or be off by any amount (so long as it isn't being deflected by ferric metals). A compass either works all the time, or it's obviously broken.

A fairly rare exception to this rule occurs in iron country, when ferric ore deposits prove more attractive to your compass than the magnetic north pole. I've encountered this problem in Michigan's iron-rich Huron Mountains, but such places are generally small enough to merely inconvenience hikers, and if you've been minding your course the effect on your compass will be noticeable immediately. You can change course to escape these effects, but in most cases a map and the surrounding terrain will provide enough information to keep you on course until your compass reads true again.

There will be many times when traveling from one place to another requires breaking your trip into sections, or legs, each of which requires a new compass bearing. Ironically, this is easier in untracked wilderness, because the first trail intersection you come to might not be the same intersection shown on your map, but a new trail created after the map was printed.

For this reason, it's imperative to have the means to calculate distances traveled with a workable degree of accuracy.

The most common map scales are 1:25,000 (1 inch equals 25,000 inches, or 694.44 yards); 1:50,000 (1 inch equals 50,000 inches, or 1,388.88 yards); and 1:62,000, which means 1 inch is equivalent to 1,722.22 yards, or just shy of a mile (1,760 yards). All map compasses have at least two of these scales printed along the edges of their see-through bases, and most also have inch and millimeter scales for making conversions.

But hikers sometimes need a way to measure actual distances on the ground for correlation with map distances. An average adult covers about 3 miles in an hour of walking—a good guideline to remember—but when circumstances demand the precision necessary to locate a cabin, mountain pass, or the correct trail, you'll need a pace counter.

The best such counter is the military model, which is essentially a heavy string with tight-fitting beads strung along its length. Unfortunately, every manufactured pace counter I've seen is calibrated to kilometers, while most maps are scaled in miles. I remedy this problem by threading 23 "beads" made from ¼-inch sections of plastic tubing with a ⅛-inch inside diameter onto a doubled shoelace. A simple overhand knot in the doubled end prevents the beads from sliding off. Another knot in the middle of the shoelace separates the beads into groups of 5 and 18, while a knot in the free ends holds them all together as a unit. Leave the shoelace at least an inch too long in either group so that you can clearly separate beads from the rest of the group by sliding them to the opposite knot. It's important to have enough friction to make the beads stay wherever you slide them.

Using the completed pace counter is simple. Starting with all the beads pushed to the inside, determine how many paces, on average, it takes you to cover 100 yards (the military says 62 paces, but I personally find that 100 steps equals 100 yards). If, for example, you determine that 75 of your paces equals 100 yards, then you'd slide one bead from the large group down to the end for each set of 75 paces. When all 18 have been pushed to the end, indicating 1,800 yards of travel, you know you've traveled approximately one mile (1,760 yards). At this point slide one bead from the smaller group to its outer end and reset all the beads in the larger group by sliding them back to the center. The process continues until all five beads in the smaller group have been pushed to the end, indicating 5 miles of travel. It's a good idea to now stop and mark your position on the map before you start the entire process over. For all its simplicity, the pace counter is surprisingly accurate, and I consider it an indispensable component of any orienteering kit.

Once, after we'd spent a whole day four-wheeling along an ancient, unmapped mountain trail, one of my companions asked me to show him our location on the map. He seemed a bit disconcerted when I told him I had no idea where we were. Sooner or later, everyone who explores the wilderness encounters this problem—you don't have to be lost to not know where you are. The solution, as I demonstrated to my anxious companion the next morning, is an orienteering exercise called triangulation, a complex-sounding technique that's actually quite simple to perform. The only requirements are two positively identifiable terrain features, a good map to reference them against, and a sighting compass that allows you to read precise bearings from these landmarks. Triangulation is of little or no use in deep forest where tall trees obscure vision,

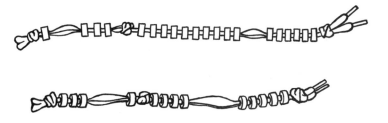

Two versions of pace counters. Top: Mile-type pace counter shows the distance traveled at 1 mile, 600 yards. Bottom: Kilometer-type pace counter showing distance traveled at 3 kilometers, 500 meters.

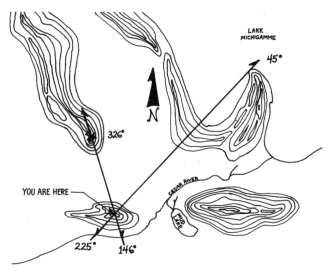

Finding your position through triangulation.

but in any open country where distant landmarks are visible, it's possible to determine within 100 yards your exact location on a map. That's important because if you don't know where you are right now—if you don't have a solid anchor upon which to base map headings—there's no way you can plot an intelligent course to anywhere else.

The first step is to find a place where you can visually identify two distant landmarks that are also identified on your map. The two points should be as far away from one another as possible. Orient your map and compass to magnetic north, making certain to compensate for magnetic declination, and sight a bearing from either point, jotting down both forward bearings and back bearings in the margins for use in the next step. Any compass can be used for triangulating, but the more precise the instrument's sighting system, the more accurate will be your calculations. This is where a prismatic (mirrored) compass shines.

Next, use the compass's protractor and straightedge to draw a line through each landmark on the map, extending these lines on the same angles as their back bearings. If your compass isn't equipped with a protractor, center its indicator post exactly on top of either reference point and use its bezel as a protractor.

You'll note that as you extend the back-bearing lines on the map back toward yourself, they draw closer together. The point where these lines intersect is your position.

Night Navigation

As much as we try to convince ourselves otherwise, few of us are unafraid to be alone in the woods at night. There are many reasons behind this fear: Humans have perhaps the lowest perception of ultraviolet light of any species, which means we can't see at night; the forest is already an alien environment where most civilized folks feel somewhat insecure in daylight; worse, all of us have been taught from childhood to fear what could be lurking in the darkness. The logical part of our brains may know that such fear is unfounded, but each of us carries a burden of childhood terror left over from tales about werewolves, vampires, and all sorts of sharp-clawed predators that wait to rend and tear unsuspecting humans in the darkness. While these stories probably sprang from an era when our distant ancestors huddled around a fire for protection from now-extinct predators that sometimes did eat them, almost every species on the planet has learned to avoid humans, none more so than in North America.

The trick to traveling at night is learning to rely less on your eyesight and more on your other senses. Your eyes will adjust better than you might think, but you must learn to use the hardness of a trail underfoot to guide your steps on moonless or cloudy nights. Condition yourself to step higher than normal to clear protruding roots and other tripping hazards. Learn to "see" movement around you with your ears, not your eyes, listening for the rushing of water, the rustling of leaves, and other audible clues. Feel for minute changes in air currents with your extremely sensitive facial skin, and learn to recognize how these tactile differences relate to changes in terrain.

Night orienteering requires a small flashlight for map reading and taking bearings, but as with any battery-powered device, you'll want to use it sparingly. I recommend using a recognizable star as a bearing point—a fixed point that you can see and follow without the aid of artificial light.

Other Orienteering Tricks

One persistent myth among outdoor lovers of all disciplines is the belief that moss prefers to grow on the northern sides of trees. The truth is that moss grows wherever conditions most favor it, regardless of direction. In fact, in the North Woods mosses actually tend toward the southern side of their hosts, away from winter's killing north wind, but always keeping to shade.

In this same vein hikers in northern and mountain states can use the tallest spruce, hemlock, or other pine tree to find their way. Since this tree will rise above the surrounding forest to face winter's full fury, any buds that sprout on its northern side will literally be frozen to death each winter. Thus the branches growing on its opposite side will always point generally south.

If you can see it, the sun is a reliable indicator of direction because, as every kid from my generation knew, east is the land of the rising sun, and cowboys always ride west into the sunset. But it's also true that our sun is directly overhead only at the planet's equator. The farther north you travel from the sun, the more southerly becomes its east-to-west arc across the sky. The opposite is true in the southern latitudes.

Chronograph-type wristwatches can also serve as compasses in a pinch, but they too rely on a visible sun to work. In the morning point the watch's hour hand at the sun, and the point where the angle

A towering pine tree can help point hikers in the right direction.

between it and the number 12 is bisected will be south. The same procedure applies when you're taking a bearing in the afternoon, except that A.M. bearings are always taken from the left (6–12) half of a watch, while P.M. bearings are read from the right (12–6) half. Watches like the Camper ($35) from Timex's Expedition line are made to exploit this potential with a rotating bezel that bears compass points in 10-degree graduations (it also has Indiglo and other useful features). This method is neither accurate or reliable enough to replace a dedicated compass—changes in latitude and cloudy days can pose problems—but if something happens to your compass, a good watch can actually help you get home.

There are also a few miscellaneous tips I can give you about using terrain features to find a route through the wilderness. For example, it's good to know that most rivers flow generally southward, and that if you follow the flow of water downstream to its outlet, sooner or later you'll run across civilization. Also, prevailing winds across North America blow generally west to east, and downhill usually leads to water.

3

Backpacking

O h, you think backpacking cures everything. After hearing this many times from my wife and friends, I realized they were right. I really do believe that a few days spent hauling your home on your back through the wilderness is a soothing remedy for most afflictions of mind, body, and soul.

Part of this belief has to do with the way being isolated from civilization forces members of a group to work together for the common good. People do seem to be drawn closer together by a 'packing trip. Parents often see admirable qualities in their offspring that hadn't been apparent behind the assumed mannerisms we all wear in society, and kids find that Mom and Dad are pretty cool after all. Verbal communication is simpler and clearer than is possible amid the noisy distractions of civilization, and the mind is free to operate on a higher, less fettered plane of consciousness.

Then there are the physical benefits of backpacking. Most obvious are the facts that no active backpackers are overweight, and few ever suffer from bad backs, knees, or leg problems. You might argue that only athletes are drawn to backpacking, but certainly the activity itself that creates them. If you want to see the most wondrous sights nature can offer, you'll have to backpack in, and that can be hard work. The spiritual benefits alone merit the effort, but those of us in the over-40 crowd can also appreciate that frequent backpacking trips can lower the chance of coronary blockage to almost zero.

Loading Up

The most common mistake made by inexperienced backpackers is loading their packs with more stuff than they can carry comfortably. Today's featherweight backpacks are light-years ahead of the canvas rucksacks we carried when I was a kid, but the activity still requires strengthening a specific set of muscles that few of us exercise in daily life. Start slowly, and always pack as lightly as conditions allow. As a general rule of thumb, the heaviest winter pack should never exceed 33 percent of its bearer's own weight, and first-timers should start with no more than 25 percent of their body weights. I figure that if I can lift the loaded pack with my stronger arm, it isn't too heavy to carry.

The most important and fundamental items of every wilderness kit are what I call the Basic Three: compass, fire-starting kit, and sharp, sturdy belt knife. With a compass, you always know which way is home; an effective fire starter guarantees you'll never freeze to death; and the infinite number of uses you'll find for a good knife will make obvious why God endowed animals with sharp teeth, claws, and hooves. In practice all of these are best carried on your person at all times, and I recommend never venturing into the woods without them for any reason.

With these most critical survival tools in hand, loading the pack continues to be based on priority. Those priorities will change in different terrain and seasons, but a sleeping system consisting of shelter from the elements and a bedroll warm enough to allow deep, restful sleep is one of several generic essentials.

Also necessary is a kit for making water safe to drink, ideally a GI canteen with metal cup for holding and boiling water, a pump-type purifier, and a bottle of iodine tablets or liquid. The mess system includes cooking vessels, eating utensils, powdered beverages, and food.

Think of your backpack as a collection of kits, each of which has been assembled to meet a specific set of needs, and each of which can be carried away as a convenient unit, without lugging the entire pack. Nylon stuff sacks work well for containing component kits, which can be color-coded for quick identification, but I've also used camera bags, fanny packs, videotape cases, soap dishes, and zipper-lock plastic bags. Use your imagination to decide what container best suits the intended application: My backpack first-aid kit, for instance, is always in a small fanny pack that I can belt on and carry at the run in a medical emergency. My "spares" kit of AA batteries, flashlight bulbs, tinder cubes, eyeglass repair kit, and other small, easily lost items is packed into a sturdy plastic videotape case with a hinged lid, held shut by a wide inner-tube rubber band.

Whatever they're contained in, all of those kits should have permanently assigned places in or on your backpack. Knowing precisely where everything is located can be a great help, especially in the dark. You don't want to be rummaging around for a first-aid kit if someone has urgent need of it, or a fire starter when you're chilled to the bone. Those and other priority items should be kept quickly accessible in external pockets if your pack has them, or otherwise segregated in places where they can be located immediately just by feel.

With your pack loaded, the next step is to fit it to your torso for maximum comfort. Today's better frame packs incorporate a variety of adjustments at the shoulders, waist, chest, and sometimes frame, making it possible to precisely fit the unit to your unique physical contours. Load-bearing straps should be cinched snug, but never tight enough to restrict blood flowing through the muscles. A properly adjusted backpack should fit like a turtle's shell, with as little strain against shoulders and back as possible. Avoid overtightening the sternum (chest) strap, because this will make your entire pack feel off balance and uncomfortable.

Once a comfortable fit has been achieved, check your loaded pack for balance. Taking full advantage of the freedom a backpacking system provides means leaving the beaten path, and this means stream crossings on slippery logs, climbing over deadfall timber, and maybe negotiating a narrow ledge in rock country. Sidling across a greasy, rain-slick log mere inches above a rain-swollen river is just one of the daily hazards that make 'packing an adventure, but falling into that water because of a sloppy-fitting, off-balance pack is just plain dumb. Avoid the almost universal mistake of loading heavy gear—especially the bedroll—on top of your pack. Keep the weight low, where it not only balances more easily but also improves your boots' traction on slippery surfaces. The final fitting process should include wearing the loaded pack while kneeling, bending at the waist, and standing on one foot— all the strange positions you'll most likely need to assume while going under, around, or over natural obstacles.

The last step is a trial run or two, an exercise I absolutely recommend for beginners, or anytime you buy a new pack. These hikes should cover at least a mile, over which any necessary final adjustments or load shiftings can be made. Even with the pack fitted as comfortably as possible, first-timers typically find themselves tiring quickly, so give yourself a little time to get into shape before actually entering the wilderness.

Trail Hazards

While backpacking is infinitely safer than driving along any road in a car, there are trail hazards that can range from mildly uncomfortable to life threatening. Virtually all are avoidable, but the worst are often not obvious, and too many folks walk into trouble because they didn't recognize potential hazards.

Wasps and Bees

Wasps, particularly the ½-inch-long yellow jackets (*Vespula maculifrons*), are one of the most important hiking hazards. Found across the United States and southern Canada, yellow jackets are fiercely protective of their nests, which are usually at or below ground level. Wasps typically nest inside a hollow log or stump, but they might also adopt underground rodent burrows near fruiting trees or shrubs.

While it's always advisable to avoid agitating bees and wasps, the danger they pose is actually negligible. In fact the yellow jacket provides a good frame of reference for evaluating the actual danger from so-called killer bees. Yellow jackets are far more numerous than African honeybees and at least as aggressive when agitated; the little wasp can also sting its victim repeatedly with potent venom, while all honeybees die after stinging just once. Considering how formidable they could be, injuries from the yellow jacket and its relatives are rare.

More than any other wasps, yellow jackets are drawn to the sweet smells of ripened apples, pears, raspberries, and other wild fruits. Strong jaws bite away the peels of large fruits, leaving shallow nibbled areas that are conspicuous by their lack of defined tooth marks. Whether still hanging or on the ground, ripened fruits and berries with shapeless excavations in them tell of a nearby yellow jacket nest, the entrance of which is generally marked by the constant traffic of at least several airborne occupants.

If you do suddenly find yourself amid a swarm of agitated wasps or bees, the best advice I can offer from hard experience is to run like the wind, and don't stop until they do. The insects won't pursue much more than 100 yards before returning to their nest, and you might escape unstung. Wasps and bees don't operate from animosity, only instinct, and their instinct is to protect the nest.

Snakes

Snakes are a source of real fear for many hikers, even though most are harmless and many are nearly toothless. All wild snakes may bite from fear, of course, but most species that do bite have no venom, and no snake wants to antagonize an adversary 50 times its own size. Forget what you've seen in the movies; an approaching human is one of the most terrifying things a snake can experience. With a crawling speed of just over 3 miles per hour, even a large snake can be overtaken at a fast walk—a fact not lost on the poor snake—and the majority of confrontations are caused by hikers who don't see cornered a snake until it turns to fight.

Strangely enough, the more aggressive a serpent acts, the greater the likelihood that it's from a non-venomous species. The large, loudly hissing eastern hognose looks very menacing with its flared cobralike hood and writhing coils, but this snake is loathe to strike because doing so

Northern water snake

would reveal that it has no teeth, and it will in fact fall "dead" if lightly tapped.

Water snakes that inhabit lakeshores and streambanks throughout the eastern United States mimic the pattern and coloration of pit vipers, especially the cottonmouth. They can be unnaturally aggressive, especially large adults with established territories. Water snakes aren't venomous, but their teeth can draw blood, and many a fisherman has been driven from a favorite hole by territorial adults that can reach lengths of more than 5 feet. A few have actually had to grab a snake by its head to unhook the curved teeth from rubber boots or waders (which are never penetrated).

Since water snakes are so often encountered along wetland hiking trails, I'll tell you how I deal with aggressive individuals that insist I leave their territories. First, I don my omnipresent leather gloves, which are impenetrable to a water snake. Then I use a long forked stick to pin the snake's head to the ground without injuring it. Finally, I pick the snake up in my gloved hands and explain to it face to face that I'm only visiting and pose no threat. When I release the snake, it returns to the water and doesn't bother me again. I like to think this technique works because the snake and I have achieved a spiritual connection, but being captured and held at the mercy of a much larger enemy is no doubt too terrifying an experience for even the most territorial water snake to chance again.

Excepting the shy coral snake of the American South, all venomous snakes in North America are pit vipers, a diverse family that ranges from the 18-inch massasauga rattler of the Northeast to the diamondback of the desert Southwest and the rattleless copperhead of the Southeast. Adventure stories notwithstanding, all of these are loathe to bite, even when antagonized, because they understand at some level that their venom won't bring down a human quickly enough to prevent fatal retribution to themselves. A coiled and buzzing timber rattler isn't looking for a fight, it's asking you to please step away because you've made it afraid. One step back is all that's required to avoid any such confrontation.

A lesson about snakes that I learned the hard way is their penchant for seeking out warm places after sunset. When I was 16, a massasauga rattlesnake slipped unnoticed into my beat-up mummy bag, which I'd left laid out under my open lean-to shelter. It could have been any kind of snake, but I happened to draw the only poisonous species in northern Michigan. It bit me, of course, and I spent the next three days shivering and sweating, my mind somewhere between delirium and deathlike sleep. It isn't an experience I'd recommend, so always zip up at least the no-see-um doors on your tent or bivy to keep out heat-seeking intruders, which can include anything from giant millipedes to scorpions and green frogs. I also suggest folding your sleeping bag into quarters when you aren't in it, then opening it completely before turning in, to dislodge any critters that might have sneaked in when you weren't looking.

Harmful Plants

Most wild plants are harmless, and a number are always suitable as human food and medicine in every foliated environment, yet hardly 10 percent have ever been studied with any enthusiasm by the scientific and medical communities.

A few, however, have historically caused grief to unwary hikers. Best known are poison ivy (*Toxicodendron radicans*) and poison oak (*T. diversiloba*), both close relatives of true sumacs. *T. radicans* is widespread throughout North America, while *T. diversiloba,* true poison oak, is found only along the Pacific Coast. Poison oak grows on a single vertical stalk to heights of 1 to 9 feet, with single leaves consisting of three oak-leaf-shaped leaflets branching in a triangular shape from a central stem. Poison ivy, which may be a long vine or clusters of individual plants less than a foot tall, is sometimes mistaken for poison oak, but whether this species matures with toothy oaklike leaves or the smooth, shiny leaves of poison ivy depends on whether it's grow-ing in sandy soil or rich forest humus. All forms develop clus-ters of white berries and leaves that turn red-orange in autumn; all are found in places where soils are moist and shaded throught their growing season.

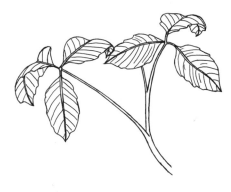

Poison ivy (*Toxicodendron radicans*)

Stinging nettle *(Urtica dioica)*

And all are a real source of misery for people allergic to the defensive toxic oils excreted through their leaves. These oils cannot be transported on a breeze; that's a myth. But they can be rubbed off by clothing, pets, and kids, then transferred to the skin of a victim, where they create what can best be described as a chemical burn. Removing the oils as quickly as possible, preferably with soap and water, will of course lessen the severity and extent of these chemical burns, but by the time many begin to suffer sympoms they've rubbed the oils onto the face and other exposed areas.

There is no cure for poisons ivy or oak, no more than there can be an instant remedy for acid burns; the damage already done must heal. On the trail jewelweed, or touch-me-not *(Impatiens capensis)*, provides a soothing treatment (see chapter 7 for more about this plant), as does Benadryl ointment, but poison ivy sufferers can count on several days of itching and misery. The best solution is learning to recognize and avoid all forms of poison oak and ivy.

A common plant in damp bottomlands and rich open forest across North America is the stinging nettle *(Urtica dioica)*, which lives up to its name while taking a toll on unfortunate hikers who often never learn the source of their misery. A tall plant—it can exceed 6 feet—stinging nettle guards itself against being eaten by acid-tipped hairs covering its leaves and stem. Like the oils in poison ivy, these tiny droplets of acid burn bare skin, causing an itchy stinging sensation on the affected area, and sometimes raising a rash of red wheals. These effects are short lived and require no treatment beyond washing the affected area, but it pays to recognize and avoid stinging nettles. It's interesting to note, though, that young nettles have long been gathered (by folks wearing gloves) as a tasty potherb; boiling neutralizes the acid.

Beating the Bugs

I'm living proof that humans have a built-in insect repellent, exuded in skin oils, that can deter bloodsucking insects as effectively as commercial repellents. The drawback is that you have to endure about a million mosquito, blackfly, sand fly, stable fly, deerfly, and horsefly bites before the metabolic repellent kicks in, and this isn't a bright prospect for most folks.

There are a good many manufactured insect repellents available from respected names like Muskol, Cutter, and Off. Nearly all use N-diethyl-m-toluamide (deet, for short) as their active ingredient, but be aware that not all of these are equal. A pump spray of, say, 16 percent deet is fine for backyard barbecues and trips to the beach, but accept nothing less than a concentration of 98 percent deet in a repellent you'll be using in the deep woods.

Regardless of which insect dope you prefer, there are plenty of outdoor lovers who can tell stories of biting bugs that drive in like crazed kamikazes despite repellents. In the old days such relentless attacks were responsible for an affliction known as swamp madness, in which northern lumberjacks sometimes went hysterical from lack of sleep and ceaseless torment. The problem is especially bad in early spring near the shorelines of marshes and lakes, where newly hatched mosquitoes and blackflies rise up in great clouds, their only objectives to feed and breed before dying.

Such circumstances demand a physical barrier between us and them, a shield that's impenetrable to the tiniest biting gnat, but lightweight, cool to wear, nonrestrictive, and as see-through as possible. Beekeeper-type head nets with wire rings that ostensibly hold the mesh away from a wearer's skin sell for about $10, but are only slightly less annoying to wear than the insects they keep out. Better, in my opinion, is a simple wide tube of netting material with an elastic band at one or both ends that permits comfortable wear with a favorite hat or cap, and stuffs into any pocket when not in use. Somebody finally began manufacturing these a few years ago (I used to have to make my own), and the retail price is about $6.

Clothing makes a big difference in bug country. Logic tells us to cover as much skin as possible, but clothing dense enough to stop a mosquito's proboscis is too hot for summer hiking. Loose-fitting, airy clothing, like a long-sleeve T-shirt that's a couple of sizes too large, allows cooling air to circulate between fabric and skin, but moves constantly with your body, leaving insects no stable biting platform. The drawback is that loose-fitting clothing is more likely to snag in thick vegetation. Authorities also recommend against wearing the color blue, which is said to attract mosquitoes.

Clothing can be further treated with pyrethrin spray, a naturally occurring toxin found in daisy flower heads that kills insects on contact. Pyrethrin, the active component of pet flea sprays, is too toxic for direct contact with human skin, but spraying it onto clothing, which is then left to dry thoroughly before wearing, offers good protection for a day or more.

4

Making Camp

Selecting a Campsite

C *amp* is another word for *home* when you're in the woods, and selection and setup of just the right site can have a lot of bearing on how enjoyable any excursion to the wilderness will be. With modern gear, like self-standing tents that need no stakes and portable cookstoves that throw no sparks, where you pitch camp isn't as critical as it was even a decade ago, but there are still a few points to consider when selecting a site.

First, of course, is to locate a nice flat area large enough to accommodate your chosen shelter and gear. The small footprint of a modern freestanding tent requires very little space, allowing camps to fit into spots that were previously too small.

But before setting up, always drop to one knee. Camping next to a stream or lake is great, but the trademark lush grasses around open waters often conceal the fact that a place is permanently moist. If your knee comes away wet, consider it a warning about what will happen to clothing and anything else left lying on it.

Conversely, beware of places that are dry and flammable, especially if you intend to build a camp fire, but even if you use a camp stove or smoke. Dried grasses, pine needles, and reindeer moss are among the best natural tinder materials on earth, and if a live spark falls onto one of them unnoticed it's entirely too possible that an uncontrollable blaze could result. For this same reason, always select a campsite that has good cover from the prevailing winds, with a source of water nearby whenever possible.

Campfires

Everything considered, I prefer a fire over a cookstove when I'm in the woods. A campfire warms both body and soul, lights the darkness, makes hot meals possible, repels biting insects and nosy wild animals, dries wet clothing, and provides an effective means of signaling for help in an emergency. The hissing blue flame of a camp stove just doesn't have the same hypnotic effect that a crackling wood fire has—even moths spurn it—and we aging backpackers can appreciate that it weighs a heck of a lot more than a fire-starting kit.

Campfires have nowadays become politically incorrect because a few ignorant campers have managed to kindle fires they didn't have the know-how and respect to manage. Used correctly, a campfire does no harm to the forest and can in fact become an island of lush new growth

The fire pit

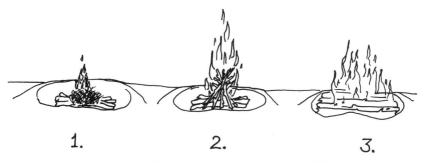

The three steps in campfire building. 1. Lighted tinder in excavated firepit. 2. Teepee of kindling. 3. Working campfire.

in a few months. I've been laying and tending fires in both woodstoves and the open since I could carry firewood, and I've never once lost control of a fire. Nor can I subscribe to the theory that a properly maintained campfire necessarily harms the forest when I see thick grasses, ferns, and other forbs springing up from the weeks-old remnant of a previous campfire. As always, respect and responsibility cannot be legislated, and how much good or harm is done by a campfire depends entirely on humans.

The first rule of campfire tending is, Always dig a fire pit. Unless you're camped on solid rock, never simply build a fire atop the ground, Always lay it in an excavated hole about 2 feet in diameter by roughly 8 inches deep. If you can accept an extra 3 pounds in your pack, an e-tool (folding shovel) makes digging a fire pit easy. A large camp knife like the SP-8 works nearly as well, and in a pinch you can use your belt knife, hatchet, or even a stick. Be prepared, however, to resharpen any cutting tool you employ for chopping through roots, sand, and dirt.

Soil excavated from the fire pit is best formed into a low wall around the pit's perimeter, where it provides an extra 4 inches or so of containment. Leave about a quarter of the wall open to facilitate cooking and fire tending. This arrangement makes it simple to refill the fire pit when you leave.

Where available, larger rocks make excellent fire borders, especially for cooking, because the stone radiates heat back like an oven. And if the weather is really cold, I'm rather fond of wrapping a fire-heated stone inside a towel or piece of clothing and then shoving it to the foot of my sleeping bag, where it keeps my toes toasty till morning.

Never place any rock you've taken from water in or near a fire. I'm obligated to repeat this warning, even if most have already heard it, because this is a mistake you might get to make only once. Like wood, stone is porous, and when it remains submerged for an extended period it absorbs water the same way. Exposing a waterlogged stone to fire causes the moisture inside it to expand rapidly in the form of steam, sometimes building sufficient pressure to explode the stone into sharp, hurtling fragments. I made this mistake one time as a boy, and although no one was injured, the experience made a believer out of me.

After excavating and walling the perimeter of the fire pit, clear a firebreak at least 4 feet wide all around it by scraping any flammable material into it, a simple task I usually perform using the side of my boot. Clearing a firebreak ensures that if embers do pop over the pit walls, they'll find nothing to ignite.

Another rule of thumb is to keep your fire as small as possible. An old Indian proverb claims that you could always identify a white man's camp because his fire was too big. A large fire is too hot for cooking, which is best done on a bed of coals; also, the bigger the fire, the more airborne embers it generates. My favorite heavyweight bivy, a Slumberjack Predator, now wears dozens of patches on its rainfly and inner netting because two fully grown fools on their first winter outing built a blazing bonfire the minute I left them alone.

Never site your fire under tree branches; always be sure it has a clear chimney to the sky. Aside from the obvious fire hazard, subjecting live overhead branches to smoke and heat does nothing to promote their health, or the public's opinion of campers in general.

Before retiring, it's a good idea to bank the campfire, which essentially means reducing it to a controlled smolder that will neither burst into flames while you sleep nor die out during the night. The easiest way to do this is to stir the coals into a level surface, then cover them completely with thick pieces of wood—even wet, half-rotted logs—placed side by side atop the coal bed. Fed by the very logs that keep it mostly smothered, the coal bed will smolder for about 10 hours, and will survive a heavy rain.

When you break camp, let the fire die down (after making morning coffee, of course), douse it thoroughly with water, and refill the hole by pushing the surrounding walls of loose soil into it. Your fire is out.

Sprinkle the filled fire pit with a concealing layer of whatever the ground cover is in that area (leaves, sand, sphagnum moss) and you'd never know a campfire had burned there. As a bonus, this practice also greatly reduces a campfire's scent, making it less likely to frighten local wildlife. The disturbed fill dirt will quickly sprout with new plant life, fed by rich nutrients from the charcoal below, and in a few months you'd never know anyone had camped there.

One legitimate concern voiced by antifire factions is that as more people are drawn to our vanishing wilderness areas, the forests will become pockmarked with dead campfires. The procedure just described addresses this, and if you camp in a place already blemished by someone else's fire, you can use and then heal over existing fire pits, too.

Getting a Good Night's Sleep

Building a Sleeping Platform

Even in warm weather it's a good idea to lay a sleeping pallet to provide a layer of insulation between yourself and the heat-absorbing earth. This is especially important in autumn, when the earth is cooling. Lightweight sleeping pads, like those I reviewed in chapter 1, are worth packing, but for many years before their invention I made my own sleeping pallets from the materials at hand.

The first step is to lay a platform of the straightest dead branches and saplings you can find placed side by side atop the snow or ground. The length of these branches depends on your own length, but it's important that they be long enough to keep both your head and feet from touching the ground.

The platform alone is enough to keep body heat from being lost into the earth, but not many find its knobs, bumps, and protrusions comfortable enough to sleep on; another layer of softer insulation is needed. Bracken ferns are my favorite bedding material, but pine needles, tall grasses, cattail leaves, or any lofty material in abundance will also work. In snow country a cushion of live pine boughs is less comfortable than ferns, but they might be the only option available, and hungry herbivores will appreciate the easy meal after you break camp.

Having a warm, cushioned bed makes sleeping under the stars more pleasant, and you can set or pitch a tent right on top, but take care

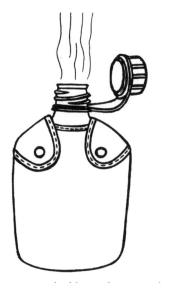

A canteen can double as a hot-water bottle—but be sure to wrap uninsulated canteens in a knit cap or cloth to prevent burns to the skin.

to remove sharp twigs and other protruberances that might poke through its floor. Finally, stomp all over the bed to break down the bumps. If a groundsheet is available, placing it over the finished mattress eliminates air circulation through the insulating spaces between itself and the earth, bumping the comfort rating of any sleeping bag down another 10 degrees or so.

Head-to-Toe Warmers

A common complaint with even good sleeping bags in winter is cold feet. Some bags compensate by placing extra insulation in the foot area, but the most important rule in avoiding an uncomfortable night of icy toes is to never wear wet socks to bed. If possible, always change into dry socks before crawling into your bag; barring this, sleep without socks. On really cold nights I pull out the liners from my pac-boots and wear them while I sleep. Wet or dry, good pac-boot liners are enough to guarantee warm feet through a night of subzero weather, and I often carry a pair of lightweight spare liners in my pack for this purpose. They also work well as camp booties for answering a late-night call of nature.

Another foot warmer I've used often for camping in the cold is the canteen hot-water bottle, made by filling a canteen with hot, but not boiling, water, then capping it tightly. Canteens with thick insulated carrying cases can be taken to bed as is, but uncovered canteens are best wrapped in a knit cap or other cloth to prevent burns from direct contact. Insulated by the sleeping bag, the hot water will generate warmth for about six hours, and as a bonus you'll have a quart of prewarmed water for beverages or drinking in the morning. Again, don't use boiling water, and always fill the bottle completely, because as trapped liquid inside the sealed canteen cools it creates a vaccuum that sucks in the outer walls and may damage your canteen.

When I was a kid, the upstairs bedrooms of our old farmhouse, heated only by a cast-iron potbellied woodstove that never managed to burn till dawn, were so cold on a midwinter morning that a glass of water from the night before would be frozen. From this, I learned to sleep with my head under the covers, recycling the heat of my breath to warm my body. This isn't a good idea with modern sleeping bags, though, because exhaled moisture inside the nonabsorbent bag evaporates to the outside, creating a cooling effect. Equally bad, the moisture left unevaporated condenses and collects on the nonabsorbent liner in droplets around your face, which is very uncomfortable.

But neither do I like sleeping with my face exposed to subfreezing air, and I hate wearing a ski mask because the eye holes always end up at the back of my head by morning. Instead, I cinch the bag's hood snugly around my face, as it's supposed to be, then cover my entire body and head with a groundsheet. This can be a blanket of any light material, like a plastic tarp or an old bedsheet. It need not be insulated; just having a dead-air space warmed by your own breath is sufficient to reduce the comfort level of any bag 10 degrees without creating a condensation problem. Enough air will come in under the edges to make suffocation impossible, but I sometimes prop up a tunnel under the groundsheet for fresh air. Breathing too high a level of exhaled carbon monoxide can make you wake up with a headache.

Makeshift Pillows

Like many middle-age backpackers, I also get a headache or a stiff neck if I sleep without a pillow to support my head. Though several companies manufacture camping pillows, carrying one in a backpack simply makes no sense to me. More logical, I think, is to fill the empty stuff sack from your sleeping bag, tent, or bivy with whatever spare clothing you have, or even with dry leaves, ferns, or grasses, and then use it as a pillow. You can also use a stuff-sack pillow to keep your butt dry when sitting around the campfire on snow-covered or otherwise wet ground.

Animals in Camp

Several years ago a friend told me of a sleepless night he and his wife had spent huddled in their tent at a remote campground while an unknown animal scavenged noisily through a bag of potato chips they'd left outside. When in the dim light of early dawn the frightened pair summoned enough courage to peek outside, they found to their embarrassment that the loud and bold marauder was a 6-ounce red squirrel.

As anyone who's "lived off the land" for a few days can tell you, with feeling, natural foods are a bland diet for folks used to eating civilized fare. It should come as no surprise, then, that many species of wild animals begin drooling when they smell spicy human foods. Fire, even burned down to embers, is a guaranteed deterrent to any wild animal, including brown bears, but as more people turn from campfires to camp stoves, more critters are finding the courage to come snooping around camp for food. With a diet consisting largely of ants, grubs, and grasses, a black bear can hardly be faulted for an attraction to corn chips and hot dogs.

The strategy most recommended for preventing hungry animals from entering camp is to hang all foodstuffs from a bag high in a tree 50 yards from camp, wash cookware immediately after use, and generally keep the area as free of food aromas as possible. All good advice for both safety and hygiene reasons, but I part company with the official doctrine of giving way to large animals bold enough to enter camp. Like my Native American mentors, I believe that surrendering your space to a bear, or any animal, is a recipe for trouble—if not for you, then for the next folks who come along.

I've never subscribed to the old adage about bears having a natural fear of people, but all large carnivores must regard humans as being at least as dangerous as themselves, for anything less than an equal is potential prey. I pack a short-barrel .22 pistol for its loud report, which can be heard for up to several miles, on the off chance that I might need rescuing someday; one shot from it into the air has never failed to set any nosy animal running. Compressed-air horns, like those used by sporting event fans to deafen one another, are at least as effective, and so are the screeching electronic personal protection alarms that many urban dwellers now carry. Loud noises are best for chasing off large, powerful animals (moose, too, may invade a camp), because they induce fear without inflicting the pain that might trigger an instinctive retaliatory attack. Mace, tear gas, and pepper spray bear repellents would be my last choices for this reason alone.

Drying Wet Clothes

As much as I wish it were otherwise, there is no clothing that will keep a backpacker dry during an extended period of rain or snow. Do what you will, you'll be wet sooner or later. What really counts is that you're warm.

But when the rain stops, or you return to camp from a long day of slogging through snow, you're going to want a way to dry those wet clothes. For this I use a drying tree—a sapling or branch, preferably dead, about 2 inches in diameter by 5 feet in length, with as many branches protruding from its main stem as possible.

Begin by cutting all the branches to pegs about 6 inches long, then sharpen the lower end to a point, so the cutoff branches are angling upward when that end is driven into the ground. If the weather is warm and dry, you can place the drying tree anywhere it will receive the maximum amount of sun. But if your source of drying heat comes from a campfire, select a spot about 5 feet from it and perpendicular to the prevailing winds—a location far enough from the fire to prevent your clothing from being burned and out of the way of wind-driven sparks.

A drying tree is a handy way to dry your clothes after a rainfall.

Drive the sharpened end of your drying tree into the earth at this spot by grasping the main body tightly in both hands and twisting back and forth while exerting a hard downward force. When you've drilled the point to a depth of 6 inches or so, and the tree feels stable enough to accept weight placed on it, you can begin hanging wet clothing from its branches. Socks, gloves, and mittens are best dried by threading them over their branches like a sleeve; shirts and jackets should be hung spread-eagle fashion from several branches; trousers dry best when hung flat and upside down, with the largest area of material nearest the most intense heat.

A common mistake is trying to dry clothing too fast—another lesson that virtually every experienced backpacker has learned the hard way at some point. A good rule of thumb is to never allow steaming clothing to become too hot to hold in your hand. The drying tree can be rotated as needed to expose the wettest clothing to the most heat, but resist the temptation to speed things along by building your fire just a bit hotter.

Keeping the Campsite Organized

One campsite habit that will serve you well is placing all of the smaller items taken from your pack in a single, obvious location before the sun sets. This is a lesson you don't want to learn the hard way, because that crunching sound underfoot may turn out to be your expensive radio receiver, or maybe something even more important. My mess kit, canteen, coffee, and spoon are left next to an easily seen bush or tree near the fire pit, the place where I'm most likely to use them. Water purifier, machete, binocular, and other items I'm likely to take with me away from camp for water, firewood, or late-afternoon animal watching are left on the ground next to my backpack, which is too obvious to trip over in the dark. Radio, eyeglass case, and midnight snacks go into the shelter. Knowing where everything is in the dark not only saves on precious flashlight batteries, but it also helps prevent tripping and falling in an environment where you can't afford to do either.

5

Campsite Cooking

One predictable phenomenon among campers and backpackers is increased appetite. Some attribute it to fresh air, but the fact that all wildlife photographers, field biologists, and other professional backpackers are physically fit is a good indication of how many calories are burned on the trail. Like a child at play, you get plenty of good cardiovascular exercise without noticing how much work you're actually doing. The end results can range from a debilitating attack of hypoglycemia (low blood-sugar level) to appetites so ravenous I've seen folks bite their own fingers while stuffing food into their mouths. In general a wilderness traveler can count on needing about double the calories he'd burn during a normal day in civilization—an important point to remember when packing food for a weeklong outing.

Campfire Cooking

While it's true that almost everything tastes better in the woods, a hot, nicely cooked meal goes a long way toward making the whole experience more pleasurable. The trick is learning to manipulate a campfire so it works most effectively as a source of cooking heat. The big secret lies in understanding that the red-hot coals of a good fire bed are roughly double the temperature generated by a kitchen range, and cooking vessels are heated from the side, as well as from the bottom.

Open flames are even hotter, and virtually anything you try to cook this way, from marshmallows and hot dogs to brown trout and rabbit, is guaranteed to get charred on its outside before being cooked through. Open flames are okay for boiling water in a hurry, but never cook food over them.

The best cooking surface consists of a solid bed of hot coals scraped from and slightly to one side of the flames. Without fuel, coals will quickly lose heat and die, so a platform of finger-thick sticks placed closely together side by side onto them provides the fuel to maintain constant heat without smothering the coals beneath. Another platform of side-by-side sticks placed atop and perpendicular to the first gives this woodsman's version of a range burner added heat and longevity.

Handling pots and other cooking vessels on a fire requires more caution than cooking in a kitchen. The wire-bale handles found on most camping mess pots are bound to become blistering hot, and probably every experienced camper has had his fingers branded at least once proving this. A pair of heavy leather work gloves, loose fitting so you can yank them off quickly when they get hot, is necessary for cooking over a campfire, but the best pot lifter I've found is a survival knife with saw teeth along its spine. Slipping the blade through the handle and sliding the bale upward until it catches on the saw teeth provides a secure and safe way to handle hot cookware, and a belt knife is one tool you should be wearing anytime you aren't in the sack asleep.

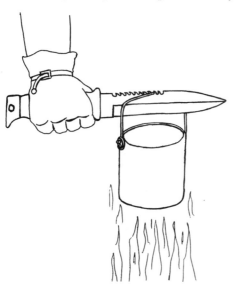

Using a survival knife and leather gloves to lift hot mess-kit pots.

While most campfire foods involve boiling and require no explanation, it's also possible to bake in a covered mess-kit pot. A wilderness cake I occasionally treat myself to is made by greasing the insides of the pot and lid with a little cooking oil, then pouring in a thick batter of instant pancake mix made with half the water recommended in the instructions. A half cup of brown sugar per quart of batter makes this cake an ideal remedy for the attacks of sugar withdrawl that can occur after several days of eating too healthy.

When baking a cake, remember that batter rises to nearly double its original volume in the pot, so don't fill it more than halfway or it may overflow the lid. Ideally the entire pot should be covered with hot coals to produce as even a heat as possible. After about 20 minutes remove the pot and check the cake by inserting a knife blade into the rising batter. If the blade comes away clean, your cake is done, but if it has wet batter on it, re-cover the pot with fresh coals and wait another 10 minutes before checking again.

Frying is a bit trickier; not only does a campfire cook have to compensate for great heat, but all backpacking mess kits are stamped of thin, lightweight metal, and poorly suited to making pancakes, frying eggs, or preparing any dish that requires a skillet. All cooking should be done over coals, never flames, but the key to regulating just the right amount of heat to cook without burning lies in keeping the pan elevated above the coal bed. Short sticks laid side by side to form a raised platform between coals and skillet keep the metal from making direct contact with coals below and help keep heat distributed more evenly over the pan's bottom. If the stick platform flames up, remove the skillet and add another platform of close-together sticks over the first to again reduce it to a smolder.

At some point it may become useful, or even necessary, to know the finer points of roasting wild game over a wood fire. Once again the most common mistake is trying to cook over too hot a fire, which chars meat on the outside while leaving the inside raw. A hot coal bed covered with a platform of long sticks placed tightly side by side provides constant low heat and a tangy taste of wood smoke. For this reason, never cook over green pine or cedar, both of which impart a taste of turpentine to foods that many find unpalatable.

Making a campfire roasting spit is simple: First, you'll need two 4-foot sticks, each with a stout fork at its upper end, to support a spit (long, straight stick) placed across them. Sharpen the unforked ends of each upright and drive them into the soil about 4 feet apart on either side of the campfire with a forceful downward twisting motion, drilling them into the ground at least 6 inches. The spit is best made from a green (not pine or cedar) sapling, to prevent it from burning through, sharpened to a point at one end and long enough to extend a foot or so past each upright when laid across them.

Spitting small four-legged food animals is best accomplished by inserting the sharpened end of the spit through a carcass's anus and out its neck. Birds are spitted the same way, but smaller fish, like bluegills and pumpkinseeds, can be speared straight through their bodies and hung in a line over the fire. Larger, long-bodied fish, like salmon or red-horse suckers, are most securely fastened by threading the spit into and back out of their bodies once, or twice if the fish is long enough.

A universal complaint among campfire chefs is that flakes of wood ash inevitably blow into any pan left uncovered, depositing "floaties" (a word from my childhood) onto the contents. You should certainly spoon out all lumps of charcoal that pop onto your food while cooking; while these are quite crunchy, most folks find the taste objectionable.

But powdered wood ash was once used widely by Native American tribes for cooking almost everything. The practice was thought to be purely ceremonial until a few years ago, when modern science finally discovered what the Indians apparently knew all along: Wood ashes break down the complex amino acids in plant cellulose, reducing them to simpler proteins that are usable by our relatively impotent human digestive systems. Hominy, a dish made from corn kernels boiled in ash water, is an ancient Native American recipe, and perhaps the only method of making whole corn digestible in our stomachs. This can be a good thing to know if circumstances limit available foods to rough, fibrous wild plants that wouldn't otherwise be suitable as food.

Washing dishes after every meal is a must in the wilderness. First, it's always a good idea to keep every campsite as free of food odors as possible to keep raccoons, opossums, and, of course, bears from being tempted by the tantalizing aromas of human food. But just as important, a film of food left in a mess kit can spoil and become poisonous overnight.

Burned-on food stuck to the inside of a cooking pot can be loosened by first filling the pot with water, then boiling it with the lid on for about five minutes. If a water source is nearby, you can use it to wash your dishes, but always refill pots with water and boil them again—along with eating utensils—to destroy any waterborne parasites that might be present.

The only accessories I carry for dishwashing are synthetic scouring pads, like 3M's Scotch-Brite brand. They don't rust like steel wool, they weigh about as much as a large feather, and they also come in handy for cleaning knives, firearms, or even callused, trail-worn feet. They make cleaning cookware an easier task, too, and can be sterilized for the next use by boiling, which does no harm to the pad.

In lieu of a scouring pad there are several natural scrubbing materials, one of which is almost sure to be at hand everywhere. Wet sand at the shorelines of lakes and streams is probably the best natural abrasive. A handful of sand rubbed over the inside of a cooking pot with a rag (to protect your fingers from being sanded) will effectively scour it clean, but several handfuls of dry sand will also work when water is scarce.

Other good scouring materials include coarse grasses, reeds, and rushes wadded into a ball and used as a scrubber. Each of these has an abrasive texture by itself, which can be enhanced by the addition of a handful of sand.

Don't worry about scrubbing off the baked-on black that accumulates on the outside of every pot and pan used over a fire. After washing off the loose soot, you'll find this black crust to be resistant to almost anything short of hammer and chisel, and not worth the effort required to remove it. Moreover, the black actually serves a useful purpose by gathering and distributing heat more evenly across a pot's surfaces. However, do pack your mess items in a fabric stuff sack or bag to keep flakes of this hardened soot from scraping loose onto other items in your pack during transport.

Camp Foods

The search for a perfect traveling food has been going on since before recorded history, and today we're still looking for the ideal lightweight, low-volume, wholly nutritious backpack food. In ancient times hunters and other long-distance hikers carried pemmican, a highly nutritious, virtually nonperishable cake or ball of ground dried meat, crushed berries (especially blueberries), and animal fat. Dried meat, or jerky, was a staple of early frontiersmen, but it lacked fat, which despite today's headlines is a vital component of any healthy diet. Trappers of old frequently greeted spring with full bellies but suffering the diarrhea and stomach cramps of an ailment they knew as rabbit starvation, an affliction in which the body has no available fat and begins to draw from its own muscle mass.

I've tried both military MREs (Meal, Ready to Eat) and several types of civilian freeze-dried meals for this book, and I cannot recommend any of them. In short their prices are too high—$5 and up— they're overpackaged, and the portions are about half of what this average woodsman wants to eat in a single meal. The nutritional value of freeze-dried meals I've seen hasn't been remarkable, and one concoction I tried, a dessert called Raspberry Crumble, was so unpalatable to me that I couldn't tolerate it even after three days and nights in a snow-packed swamp.

Rice is by far the best all-around backpacking food I've ever found, and there are a good many Vietnam War veterans from either side of that conflict who can vouch for the health and strength of humans whose diet consists mainly of this grain. Eaten alone, a handful of boiled rice makes a nutritious and filling, if bland, meal, but the real beauty of this inexpensive water-grass kernel is that it makes an excellent base for so many other dishes. A pot of rice boiled with a can of finely chopped peaches is the traditional camp breakfast in my family, but ½ pound of raisins, prunes, or any dried or canned fruit will work equally well, depending on your personal taste. Fish, meat, any wild vegetable, or any combination of these works to add variety, vitamins, and minerals. The number of possible recipes that use rice as a base is limited only by imagination and the availability of supplemental ingredients.

An ongoing debate among civilized rice eaters concerns which type is the better food, natural brown rice or bleached vitamin-enriched white rice. In my world this is a moot point, because experience has proved that either will keep a person healthy indefinitely, and whatever your rice doesn't provide can be obtained from other ingredients. If you can't decide which is better, mix the two together. White rice generally retails for about $1 per pound, brown rice about double that.

Ramen noodles are another of my favorite backpack foods. A cup of hot noodle soup is a satisfying lunch on a cold day, and like rice, ramen noodles make a good base to which fish or meat can be added. The price of a 3-ounce single-serving package averages about 20 cents, making ramen noodles a best buy among backpacking foods.

Macaroni and cheese is another common dish that lends itself readily to backpacking. A single box retails for about $1 and will feed at least two hungry hikers. Because most brands are packaged in a cardboard box, I recommend protecting them from moisture in a zipper-lock bag.

Potatoes, too, are available on your grocer's shelves. Betty Crocker is one brand of dehydrated au gratin and scalloped potatoes I've backpacked with, and these almost seem designed to function as wilderness table fare. Simply dump the contents into a pot, add the prescribed amount of water, cover, and let simmer until the potatoes have reconstituted to their original consistency. A single box of dehydrated potatoes retails for under $3 and will feed two people, or you can add fish, meat, vegetables, even boiled rice. To save space in your pack, I recommend dumping the cardboard-boxed spuds into a zipper-lock plastic bag or plastic peanut butter jar (one of my favorite backpacking containers)—along with the printed instructions, if necessary.

Whatever foods you carry, you're sure to want spices to pep them up. Salt and pepper carried in screw-top plastic bottles that originally held other spices are basic, but I'm also fond of chili powder, cayenne pepper, Tabasco sauce, and bouillon cubes. Small sealed containers (emptied plastic spice bottles and the like) of brown sugar, cinnamon, powdered milk, and powdered eggs further open the possibilities for creative campfire chefs without adding much weight to the backpack.

Mess Kits

When I was a kid, an old enamel saucepan sufficed as a mess kit, and I still teach my survival students the value of a metal can or even a hubcap as an emergency cooking vessel. But backpacking cook sets, like everything else, have benefited from advances in metallurgy and manufacturing technology in recent years.

By strange coincidence, the most practical and functional field chow kit is also the least expensive. Kidney-shaped pot-type kits with

Re-use plastic spice containers to bottle and bring your favorite cooking spices.

bale (wire) handles, covers that double as bowls, and a nested folding-handled dish are standard issue for European armies whose soldiers might be called on to fight without resupply, eating from the land as they go. Unlike the U.S. military's mess kit, these are made for cooking as well as standing in chow lines, and they work exceptionally well for backpackers whose meals are usually prepared by boiling. These kits are most easily found through military surplus mail-order outlets like Major Army Navy Surplus. They weigh a backpackable 17 ounces and retail for an affordable $4 each.

One high-tech example of how far campware has come from the heavy cast-iron skillet of early trappers and voyageurs is the BlackLite gourmet cook set from Mountain Safety Research (see the source list on page 51). Made from black anodized aluminum with grooved bottoms that promote even heating and prevent sliding, the set consists of a pot lifter, a 1½-liter pot, a 2-liter pot, a deep skillet, and a snug-fitting lid that covers all three vessels. Black outer surfaces absorb heat more efficiently than bare metal, and grooved bottoms increase

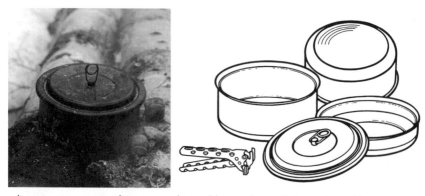

The MSR (Mountain Safety Research) Backlite cookset is lightweight and has a non-stick coating for easy cleaning.

the surface area being heated, both features designed to make the most of cookstove fuel.

But I'm especially fond of the generously thick nonstick coating MSR has applied to each pan's interior cooking surfaces. Like nonstick kitchenware, the coating requires the use of nonmetal utensils, but it makes washing dishes a whole lot less tedious. Best of all, the entire cook set nested in its stuff sack (included) weighs a mere 24 ounces and costs just $43. The basic set without skillet weighs 18 ounces and costs $33. Or you can purchase the skillet alone for $10.

Mess-Kit Carrying Tips

Whether you use your mess kit over an open fire or camp stove, you're sure to want a stuff sack to put it into for carrying. Baked-on soot is a fact of life for camping cookware, and beyond washing away the loose soot on their outsides, scrubbing mess kits down to bare metal isn't worth the effort. Aside from this, fire blackening actually increases the amount of heat transferred to the vessel. The problem is that this black coating does flake off inside the backpack. A nylon stuff sack with drawstring closure protects other gear that doesn't work better when blackened, and provides a convenient way to haul dirty dishes to a nearby stream for washing. While you're there, you can even wash the sack, then hang it from a tree to dry.

When packing your mess kit away, remember that it too can be packed with stuff like ramen noodles, instant oatmeal, spice bottles, or any other food item small enough to fit. This practice not only makes the most efficient use of space where space is a limited commodity, but also keeps food and cook set together in a unit.

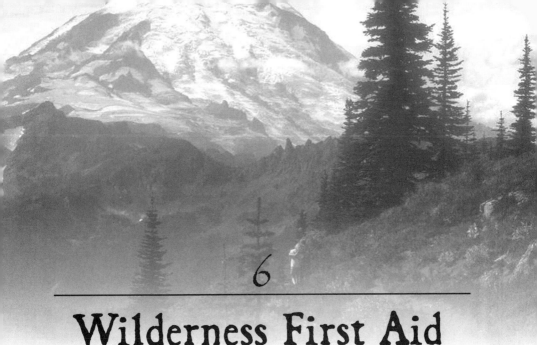

6

Wilderness First Aid

I t was the first week of March, and while daytime highs soared into
the 40s, 2 feet of slowly rotting hardpack snow remained on the
ground, rehardened each night by near-0 temperatures. I'd already been
in the swamp for three days when my best friend, Dar, joined me, clank-
ing into camp carrying a Coleman lantern, an ashcan-size catalytic
heater, and 2 gallons of fuel. Both are great appliances for ice fishing
and snowmobile jamborees, but neither has any place in a minimalist's
backpack, where every ounce must balance against the energy expended
to haul it. Dar ignored my remarks to this effect and hauled everything
inside his roomy A-frame shelter, where he kept the heater burning
despite my nagging about how much dragging out his dead, asphyxi-
ated body would inconvenience me.

Two days later I was standing next to the fire pit drying my damp
clothing while the sunset caused air temperatures in the lowlands to
plummet 20 degrees in half an hour. Dar was inside his shelter, where I
could hear him fooling with that damned heater.

Suddenly I heard that distinctive *fwoof* sound made by highly
combustible liquids when they ignite. Dar burst from the door of his

shelter, eyes wide with terror and a flaming plastic bottle in his out-stretched right hand. His heavy wool shirt was aflame from wrist to shoulder, and even his knit cap was spotted with burning fuel. Our eyes locked for an instant, and it appeared that he was balanced on a thin edge between blind panic and logical action.

"Dar," I yelled, "roll. Roll." He obeyed automatically, falling with an audible thud onto the refrozen hardpack. The still-flaming fuel bottle skittered harmlessly across the hard crust as Dar rolled back and forth with enthusiasm, extinguishing himself in seconds. I went to work putting out the inferno inside his shelter, but his sleeping bag and a few other more or less indispensable items suffered some degree of damage before they were extinguished.

Most serious was Dar's right hand, which had been holding the fuel bottle. Heavy wool clothing had protected his arm and head, but the back of his unshielded hand looked right out of a horror movie. The flesh was red and wet, and pieces of grayish dead skin hung from it like tattered rags. Dar bore his injury with a toughness born of long experience handling pain (he'd broken his neck in a motorcycle accident five years previously), but it was obvious that he'd felt better.

I pulled the GI first-aid kit from his somehow intact ALICE pack and dumped the contents onto his mummy bag, which had a 10-inch hole burned through its outer shell at the foot but was otherwise undamaged. If you need to quickly plug a bullet wound in combat, the GI kit might suffice, but there were few items among its contents that I'd consider useful. So I grabbed the homespun fanny-pack first-aid kit from my own pack and, after cutting away the dead skin with scissors and tweezers, applied analgesic and antibiotic ointments. Finally, I gave Dar four 200-milligram ibuprofen tablets for the pain.

Two days later, when Dar made it back to civilization and a doctor (his wife insisted on the latter), the M.D. pronounced his wound as well cared for as it could have been with "proper" medical attention. He asked twice how such thorough treatment could have come from a field first-aid kit in the middle of a swamp.

Thirty years of witnessing and committing acts that have had regrettable consequences has left me a little paranoid about medical emergencies. Most of the time a first-aid kit is just extra weight in your pack, but with a good one you have the tools to keep an injury victim alive, as well as the means to reduce potentially serious wounds to minor inconveniences. Even if you travel in a group, civilization and medical attention can be a very long way off to someone with a twisted or broken ankle, to a day hiker who discovers suddenly that he's allergic to bee stings, and especially to victims of waterborne illnessess. Caution and respect go a long way toward preventing injuries, and most mishaps are minor anyway, but I wouldn't think of 'packing into any remote area without a practical, functional medical kit. Just in case.

Wilderness First-Aid Kits

I wish there were a ready-made first-aid kit that I could recommend, but despite many attempts by the Red Cross and others, manufactured medical kits typically contain more useless than useful items for real life in the boondocks. If you want a really functional first-aid kit, you have to put it together yourself. Packing your own first-aid kit allows you to tailor the medical gear inside to different environments, letting you eliminate items you're sure won't be needed to make room for stuff you're more likely to find useful. Following is a roster of first-aid tools that I believe are generic to every environment. Add to them as you deem necessary to better suit your kit to a particular terrain or season.

Most-Recommended First-Aid Items (Full Kit)

Bottle of 100 ibuprofen tablets, 200 mg (painkiller)

12 cold capsules—your preference

12 capsules Imodium A-D (antidiarrheal)

12 glucose tablets

Small bottle of multivitamins

Roll of 1-inch-wide self-adhesive safety tape

Tube of triple-antibiotic ointment

Two 3-foot lengths of surgical latex tubing

Liquid iodine antiseptic

Butterfly sutures (Steri-Strips)

Small scissors

Toenail clippers

Tweezer

Small folding razor knife

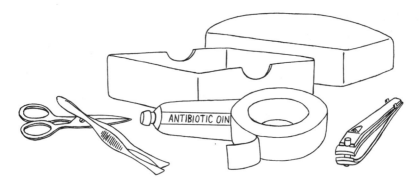

A bar-soap container doubles as an easy-to-carry and economical receptacle for first-aid supplies.

For backpackers and daypackers, that's about as thorough as you need to be. Already having the Basic Three—survival knife, fire starter, and compass—gives you the means to warm an injury victim in shock, to cut splints, and to make a cross-country trek for help. The first-aid kit itself serves to address more immediate concerns, like closing a wound to infection, stanching blood flow, and making those in pain more comfortable. The multivitamin, which should be chewed to ensure complete absorption, is a preventative measure that helps keep your immune system strong.

An advantage of putting together your own first-aid kit is that you also have a great many options for containing it. Pocket kits made from a two-piece plastic soap dish slipped inside a GI compass pouch and containing just the essentials—Band-Aids, butterfly sutures, antibiotic ointment, tweezers, and so on—are ideal for hikers and hunters. Plastic videotape boxes have enough inside space to pack more first-aid supplies than most will ever need, while their hard walls serve to protect the contents from being crushed inside a backpack. Small fanny packs make excellent traveling first-aid kits when you need to go to the victim, and they come in a variety of sizes, styles, and colors.

Treating Wilderness Afflictions and Emergencies

Cuts and Abrasions

The most common injuries in the out-of-doors are cuts and abrasions, many the result of handling sharp cutting tools, and most of these on the hands and fingers. Superficial scrapes and cuts that don't fully penetrate the skin to underlying muscle or bone are best cleansed with soap and water, disinfected with antibiotic ointment, and, finally, covered to prevent contamination while the skin recloses for a day or two. You can forgo the soap by washing iodized canteen water over the injury, and the infinitely useful safety tape serves very well as quick-to-apply bandage that resists water and dirt better than conventional Band-Aids.

Deeper, bleeding cuts can be stanched by first wrapping several turns of safety tape snugly—not tightly—around the injury from either side, pushing the opened skin back together, and then sealing the wound over with several more turns of safety tape. Note that this is a preliminary bandage, applied immediately, and its real purpose is to stop the flow of blood from the wound until it can clot and begin closing on its own. If after a few hours the extremity turns cold or numb from lack of circulation, remove the preliminary bandage with scissors and rebandage with looser turns of safety tape over antibiotic ointment.

While I've used the above technique many times to treat cuts to the fingers that were deep enough to require stitches, always with good results, deep or long gashes on larger extremities like the arms, legs, and torso need better closure. For these, butterfly sutures, so called for their shape and extremely adhesive backing, are your best bet for pulling both sides of a wound together. If hair is abundant in the area, it may have to be shaved to expose enough skin for proper adhesion. Maintaining direct pressure on an injury will slow or completely stop bleeding during the closure process. If direct pressure isn't feasible, a tourniquet of latex tubing, cord, strapping, or a belt tied above the wound will restrict blood flow to the area while you work to close it, but cutting off the blood supply to any wound is always a last resort.

Never attempt to sew shut any wound with any type of needle or thread. Stitching is the best method of closure, but chances are too good that infection-causing organisms will be introduced into a wound during the operation. Enough people have contracted gangrene to make do-it-yourself stitches a bad idea in the field.

Minor cuts, abrasions, burns, and punctures are best tended by cleansing and treating with antibiotic ointment, then leaving the wound open to scab over. A thick bandage can be applied to prevent painful bumps or contamination by foreign matter while on the trail, but injuries should otherwise be exposed to open air as much as possible.

Snow Blindness

Snow blindness is a temporary but debilitating affliction caused by subjecting the unprotected eyeballs to bright, reflected sunlight for a period of time sufficient to cause the optic nerves to shut down from synaptic overload. The term derives from the fact that bright sunlight against the highly reflective surface of a snowfield poses the greatest danger, but "snow" blindness can also occur on water or in open desert. The blindness isn't dangerous by itself, but to be suddenly without vision for 24 hours or more can be life threatening in the wild.

The best defense, of course, is to prevent snow blindness from occurring, and this isn't usually difficult. A wide-brimmed hat or visored cap pulled low over the eyes is usually adequate, as are sunglasses and tinted goggles. Mosquito head nets are also effective for diffusing sunlight that reaches the eye, as is the time-honored slitted mask of birch bark tied over the eyes.

Symptoms that precede the onset of snow blindness include severe headaches caused from squinting; sore, scratchy eyes; and bright spots dancing across the victim's vision. If you experience any of these, wrap or otherwise shield your eyes with whatever is available. Once it's contracted, the only solution for snow blindness is to wrap the eyes to protect them from further trauma, and to wait. The problem generally cures itself within a day or so, but until that time count on being effectively stranded.

Dehydration

Dehydration is a common and potentially dangerous concern at all times of year. Perhaps the worst and most immediate result of not keeping the renal system well flushed is a debilitatingly painful kidney infection. In subfreezing weather, when moisture is absorbed from the skin, wicked away by clothing, and dissipated invisibly into dry, frigid air, the danger of dehydration is heightened because victims often don't feel hot and thirsty. The same can apply to open desert, where hot, arid air absorbs perspiration before it can wet the skin.

Early warnings that you aren't drinking enough water include dark yellow to coffee-colored urine, usually accompanied by a strong odor, and sometimes by constipation so severe that feces must be removed from a victim's colon with the fingers. Coffee or tea can help relieve the latter before it becomes painful, but the best remedy for both is to increase your consumption of fresh water until symptoms clear. Estimates of how much water a person should consume per day vary, but if the urine is clear and stools are soft, you're drinking enough.

Frostbite
Frostbite is a painful result of exposing naked skin to subfreezing air temperatures until it begins to freeze and the moisture in it turns to ice crystals, much the same as the ice crystals that form in a frozen hot dog or piece of fruit. Frostbite can occur anywhere on the body, but the nose, cheeks, chin, ears, fingers, and toes are most susceptible, because they are normally the least protected.

The first symptom at the onset of frostbite is a stinging of exposed skin, almost a burning sensation, that's sometimes referred to as frostnip. No real skin damage has occurred at this point, and if the afflicted area is rewarmed immediately it will recover completely. If you haven't experienced this recovery process, be prepared to endure considerable pain in the fingers and toes as blood flow is restored to them. Over-the-counter analgesics can help reduce the pain, as well as thin the blood and speed circulation, but narcotic-type painkillers that slow the metabolic system—and the rewarming process—are to be avoided.

Immersing frozen hands and feet in a bucket of warm water is the most effective remedy for frostnip and frostbite, but never soak an afflicted extremity in water warmer than body temperature (98.6 degrees Fahrenheit) or you might create further tissue damage. For the same reason, never massage frostbitten areas. The Eskimo trick of placing a victim's hands or feet inside the coat of another and directly against the bare skin of the abdomen is very effective, if uncomfortable for the person administering the treatment. Of course, this should never be attempted by anyone who feels cold himself.

The next stage of frostbite is numbness and a marked whitening of the skin, caused by formation of ice crystals within the outer epidermal layers. At this point you've definitely sustained some tissue damage, and necrosis—a sloughing away of dead flesh—will result during recovery, which has now become a healing process. In the worst cases, where extremities like fingers and toes have been frozen through, necrosis of the entire digit can result, followed by gangrene and making amputation necessary. Again, first-aid treatment is limited to gently rewarming the affected area right away, but frostbite victims should immediately seek medical attention.

Hypothermia

Hypothermia is the most common and dangerous of cold-weather maladies, because it can occur in almost any geographical location, in any season. It wasn't long ago that three U.S. Army Rangers, arguably the best-trained soldiers on earth, died from exposure in Florida's Everglades. A human without some protective clothing or outside warmth is at risk of "freezing" to death after prolonged exposure to temperatures as warm as 50 degrees Fahrenheit. A drop of just 8 degrees in a victim's external body temperature is potentially fatal, and when the temperature of vital organs drops to 70 degrees, death is almost certain.

It follows, then, that the colder outside temperatures are, the greater the risk of contracting hypothermia, and the more important it is to dress for the environment in which you'll be traveling. Bear in mind that temperature drops of 30 degrees or more are common after sunset, and that even a warm rain makes the ambient temperature feel 20 degrees colder. A lightweight day or fanny pack with dry wool socks, a knit sweater, and gloves (as well as basic survival tools) should be an integral part of every outdoorsman's kit, no matter how warm daytime temperatures may be.

The first symptom of hypothermia is violent shivering, involuntary muscle spasms designed to increase the flow of warm blood through a victim's body. The onset of shivering may creep up slowly over several hours, or it might occur suddenly, as when an ice fisherman plunges into frigid water. The treatment in any case is to remove all wet clothing, wrap the victim in a sleeping bag or several blankets to prevent further heat loss, and then rewarm the body. A shower or bath is ideal for restoring lost body heat, but in the woods a warm fire usually suffices.

Chemical hand-warmer packets held in place by elastic bandages over the kidneys, underarms, wrists, and other places with maximum blood circulation help speed recovery. Likewise, a capped canteen filled with warm water and held to the abdomen of a blanket-wrapped victim serves to prewarm blood passing to all points of the body. Forcing a victim to walk can overcome hypothermia at its onset, but in severe cases the victim may experience crippling cramps or even lose consciousness.

Burns

Burns are an all-too-common injury among campers, whether from a fire or a camp stove. With luck and good sense, you'll never have an experience like the one I related at the start of this chapter, but burns are a part of life in the woods.

First-degree burns in which the skin doesn't immediately blister can be treated with an antiseptic-analgesic spray, like Bactine. Second-degree burns that blister immediately are best lanced and drained to relieve uncomfortable pressure, then coated with antibiotic ointment and bandaged for a couple of days to prevent contamination and infection. Third-degree burns in which the upper skin layers have been burned through and charred must be cleaned of potentially infectious debris—a painful experience for the victim—then coated with antibiotic ointment and bandaged. Take ibuprofen as needed (per manufacturer's instructions, of course) for pain, and change the bandages at least once every two days. Aside from this, the only cure for any burn is to let it heal.

Insect Bites

Insect bites are another fact of life in the wild. No insect repellent yet devised will completely stop hunger-maddened mosquitoes and black-flies during a spring hatch. Muskol lotion with 100 percent deet has been my preference since its introduction, but be assured that there will be places where biting insects disregard any repellent. Aside from the itchy wheals their bites leave behind, insect vampires further torment their victims by flying into the ears, eyes, and nostrils, up sleeves and pants legs, down the collar, and through any hole that offers access for their tiny bodies.

The good news is that at least some humans have a natural repellent, exuded through the skin, that drives off biting insects. The bad news is that you have to be bitten many, many times for this metabolic repellent to activate. But you can decrease your body's appeal to insect vampires by taking two to three capsules each of garlic and vitamin B_{12} per day. Either or both of these supplements help make your own perspiration distasteful to insects.

The best defense against any type biting bug is a physical barrier. Olive-drab head nets made from fine mosquito (no-see-um) netting protect the head and neck without obsuring vision, help camouflage the face, and retail for about $6 from most outdoor retailers (I buy the netting and sew my own). With or without the head net, a brimmed hat is necessary to hold the mesh away from your face and to keep the bugs—especially deerflies—from getting tangled in your hair. Long trousers with bloused (tied) ankles keep ticks and other bugs from climbing inside your pants legs, while long sleeves with snug-fitting cuffs are a must in areas of heavy mosquito or blackfly infestation. Clothing should be loose fitting to help keep probing biters from reaching the skin, and made from tightly woven ripstop fabric, which most bugs find impenetrable. Pretreating these garments with your preferred insect repellent gives the most potent, longest-lasting protection but also leaves scents that can alert animals to your approach from up to several hundred yards.

Snakebites

Snakebites are an unlikely possibility that many hikers find disproportionately terrifying. In truth no snake wants to tangle with an enemy 50 times its own size. With few or no weapons and a top speed of about 4 miles per hour, serpents the world over have learned to rely on stillness and skin camouflage to escape large predators. Good eyesight and acute sensitivity to ground vibrations usually give snakes advance warning of your approach, but the tendency of the cold-blooded creatures to nap on hard, sun-warmed surfaces—like footpaths—frequently brings them into contact with people. Probably most snakes escape or go undetected, but sometimes a hiker's steps stray close enough to frighten them.

Smaller snakes, including the extremely neurotoxic coral snake of the American Southwest, always try to escape, and bite only when handled. Larger snakes may react more aggressively when alarmed, coiling, hissing, and even striking, with nonvenomous species typically exhibiting the most aggression to compensate for a lack of fangs. Many, like the water snakes, mimic the pattern and coloration of cottonmouths and rattlesnakes, but while some can inflict a painful bite that breaks the skin, the wound poses no real danger beyond infection. A few, like the large, ferocious-acting eastern hognose, are completely harmless, lacking the teeth to back up their posturing.

The most certain method of escaping the classic Hollywood dilemma of a coiled and rattling pit viper is to simply take a step backward—remember, no snake wants to bite you. Hikers should keep alert for long, sticklike bodies stretched across trails in the morning and afternoon; in places where temperatures remain above 70 degrees Fahrenheit at night, all hiking should be done during daylight. Contrary to myth, snakes are not attracted by the body heat of sleeping humans, and none can penetrate a zipped-closed tent or bivy.

If you are bitten, the first step is to examine the bite. All pit vipers, from massasauga and timber rattlers to diamondbacks and sidewinders, inject venom through two long, hollow fangs that leave distinctive paired puncture wounds. The puncture marks turn red and begin to swell immediately, accompanied by a sharp, sometimes painful burning sensation.

Begin field-treating a venomous bite by applying a tourniquet to constrict, but not completely cut off, blood flow above it and to slow the spread of toxin through the victim's body. Loosen the tourniquet if the victim complains that it's causing pain. If you have a plunger-type extractor that employs strong suction to draw snake (also spider and bee) venom through the same holes it was injected through, use it immediately. Case histories have shown that suction extractors can greatly reduce the amount of venom that actually gets into the victim's body. Finally, get the victim to a hospital as quickly as possible. Depending on where the bite is located, the first-aid treatment applied, and the amount of venom injected, victims might not feel a systemic reaction (shivering, sweating, fever, thirst, hallucinations) for several hours. The farther a victim can make the trip under his own power, the easier it will be on everyone concerned.

Be warned that doctors now advise against using the old cut-and-suck technique as first aid for snakebites. It causes excessive tissue damage to areas already afflicted by venom, and it greatly increases the risk of a secondary infection. If you don't have a venom extractor, do nothing to the bite.

Sprains

Sprains are a common injury among folks who hike the backcountry. Just having a stone roll sideways underfoot while you're humping a 50-pound pack can result in a sprained ankle or knee, perhaps even a broken leg. Good, properly tied footwear goes a long way toward preventing injury to the vulnerable ankles, but twists and sprains do occur, and they can ruin an outing.

Never try to force yourself to walk on a leg injury, or you might turn a short recovery into a longer one. I recommend making camp right where the injury occurred, and soaking the affected leg in a cold stream or lake for several hours if one of these is at hand. After a good night's rest, wrap the ankle and foot, leaving heel and toes exposed, with several snug turns of 2-inch-wide safety tape (my preference) or as many turns of elastic bandage as you can apply and still get your boot on. Wear thick socks and tie the boot onto the injured foot a bit more tightly than normal to increase support. Again, never force yourself to go on, and stop to rest whenever the sprain becomes painful.

Hypoglycemia

It was March 30, three days into a scheduled eight-day outing that had so far kept my 15-year-old nephew and I saturated under incessant cold rains punctuated by blinding lightning, howling winds, and large trees that shook the earth when they fell. We'd just rolled out of our sleeping bags to another dark morning of pounding raindrops that dampened our enthusiasm for boondocking only slightly less than they did our clothing.

Spring rains are cold in northern Michigan. My nephew Josh was standing with his back to our campfire, warming himself and trying in vain to dry his backside while his front side absorbed more rain. Suddenly the young fellow's eyes rolled back in his head and he just sat down hard on top of the mound of red-hot coals our campfire had generated. I watched in horror as his right hand, protected only by a soaked fleece glove, completely disappeared into that crimson inferno.

Time slows to a crawl during such moments, and before that blazing heat could penetrate his wet clothing and gloves (thank God his hands had been cold), I'd somehow yanked the 235-pound teenager back onto his feet. The jolt brought Josh to his senses with no harm done except for the decade or so of life it cost his poor old uncle. We were both exceptionally lucky; at top speed, I couldn't have left and returned with proper medical help in less than four hours.

I didn't need a medical degree to know why my nephew had fainted; I'd seen and experienced the same too many times not to recognize the symptoms of hypoglycemia, a debilitating drop in blood sugar common among backpackers during acclimation to a cold environment. Civilized humans are well fed, and not used to drawing from fat reserves when the levels of ready energy in the bloodstream become too low to power muscles at peak efficiency. Combine the heavy exertion of wilderness backpacking with weather that forces the metabolic furnaces to run full steam, and our bodies can experience a sort of shock. As a defense against starvation, the brain begins powering down bodily systems to conserve energy, creating symptoms that can range from general fatigue, chills, nausea, and depression to outright fainting.

I regret knowing that in a prolonged survival situation these symptons pass as your body adapts to burning its own reserves, but for weekend campers the logical solution is to replace depleted blood sugar levels immediately. In my nephew's case I started by getting a mug of hot chocolate into his belly, which relieved his feelings of fatigue and disorientation within minutes.

But the rush of energy provided by simple sugars is merely a Band-Aid, not a cure, for the root cause of hypoglycemia. The best solution is to give your body the fuels it requires to function smoothly at normal metabolic levels during periods of extraordinary activity. Like dry poplar logs in a woodstove, simple sugars burn fast and hot, but what an active outdoorsman needs is the dietary equivalent of hardwood logs. Foods that contain many calories, but in a form that will be consumed more slowly and steadily in a sort of time-release effect, are the best choices. Starchy foods of all kinds meet these criteria, and because so many of them are also dehydrated, lightweight, and inexpensive, they also make great trail fare (see chapter 5).

Hypoglycemia is also a concern at bedtime, and stoking the metabolic furnace with good, long-burning fuel just before turning in does a lot to keep you warm during the night. In civilization eating before bedtime contributes to weight gain, but a camper needs the extra energy.

Useful Wild Plants

No study of woodslore can be complete without learning about at least some of the many wild plants that have provided our species with food, medicine, and construction materials throughout its rise to dominance. Millions of years of adaptation and evolution have resulted in a staggering mix of genetic combinations and molecular compositions that modern science has only begun to investigate, or understand. About 10 percent of the earth's plant life has ever been tested for anything at all, so we can only guess at what miracles might yet be hidden under the canopy of our planet's vanishing forests, or even in our own backyards.

Fortunately, what we do know covers hundreds of plants worldwide that have verified usefulness as food, medicine, or workable raw materials. Covering all of the known plants is worthy of volumes in itself, and well beyond the scope of a single chapter, so I've limited this section to just the most useful and common in North America. Be aware, however, that many of these have counterparts on other continents, and some species are identical throughout the world, so in many cases the information presented here also applies globally.

Common Plantain (*Plantago major*)

This ubiquitous ground plant is the bane of gardeners and suburbanites everywhere—which is ironic, because it was purposely transported from the Old to the New World with the first pioneers. The genus name *Plantago* is a Latin word that translates to "sole of the foot," but Native Americans also knew it as whitefoot, because, it was said, the plant grew everyplace a white man walked.

One of the better wild potherbs, plantain was once cultivated for its edibility, wide range of suitable growing soils, and remarkably fast growth rate. Cutting a mature plant to its roots results in a whorl of new growth within 48 hours, and a mature plant in about a week.

With leaves richer in vitamins A, C, and iron than spinach, and tall, fleshy seedpods rich in essential B vitamins, plantain is an important food plant in any survival situation. But maybe more important, it grows virtually everywhere, from cracks in city sidewalks and driveways to lawns, meadows, and open swamps.

Mature plantain leaves may be eaten raw, but they're stringy (young leaves are best), and the seedpods are bland. But boiled and seasoned as a potherb, and perhaps added to existing staples, the entire plant is palatable, nutritious, and digestible.

Plantain is also an important plant for medicinal reasons. A larger Asian counterpart has long been cultivated for its seeds, which are processed and sold commercially under the familiar name Metamucil. A poultice of crushed leaves bandaged over bee stings, spider bites, or insect bites reduces swelling, speeds healing, and helps alleviate pain. Eating several raw seedpods per day keeps vitamin B levels high in the outer skin, which works to discourage biting insects.

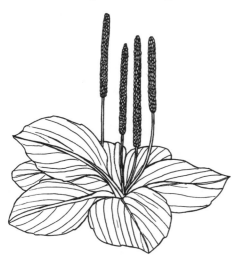

Common plantain (*Plantago major*)

Common Burdock
(*Arctium minus*)

Common burdock (*Arctium minus*)

Nearly everyone has seen burdock growing in abandoned lots and fields, along ditches, and in almost every sunny place from northernmost Canada to Mexico. Resembling nothing so much as it does a hairy version of the rhubarb plant, burdock was an important food source when America was wilderness, and even today an Asian cousin, great burdock (*A. lappa*), is cultivated in China for its large, starchy taproot.

Every part of a burdock plant is edible and digestible at all stages of growth, but palatability appears to be largely a matter of personal taste. The thick white taproots look and taste similar to a parsnip, except a bit chewier, and high levels of starches make them nutritious survival fare. The flowering burrs, with their fuzzy purple blossoms, are marginally palatable and nutritious raw or cooked. Some folks like to eat the cores of large stems after peeling the outer rind away, but I find them too bitter. One fellow told me that batter-fried burdock stems were a staple in his family during boyhood, but I haven't tried that recipe.

Tall Goldenrod (*Solidago altissima*)

This most common of the more than 50 goldenrod species found throughout North America (most of them east of the Rockies) is seldom recognized as the valuable potherb it is. A close cousin, sweet goldenrod (*S. odora*), has long been a staple of survival manuals, but tall goldenrod is just as good to eat and usually a lot more plentiful.

The choicest part of tall goldenrod is its immature top, a succulent, leafy cluster with a pungent aroma that's somewhere between licorice and carrots. Though these tops are tender enough to eat raw, some find

Tall goldenrod (*Solidago altissima*)

the taste too intense (they give me heartburn); they're best boiled before eating to dull both effects. Tall goldenrod continues to sprout throughout the summer months, so immature tops are even more valuable for their availability.

In late summer many tall goldenrod plants develop green ball- or egg-shaped bulges just beneath their budding tops. These fleshy balls of tissue are created when a tiny grub bores into the plant's stem to create a winter home in which it will mature. The fleshy balls are an odd scarring reaction that first serve as a food source for the developing grub then, after the plant dies, as a warm barrier of insulation against winter's cold.

Green goldenrod balls may be eaten raw, but like the leafy tops they have a strong parsnip and licorice taste that can be reduced to toleration by boiling them until tender. Boiled and seasoned, goldenrod balls are one of nature's finest vegetables. You may leave the grub inside, for it too has food value, but most folks prefer to quarter the fleshy balls and remove their residents.

Wild Leek (*Allium tricoccum*)

Wild onions are found throughout North America, and while each member of the genus *Allium* prefers a specific growing environment, there's enough diversity among family members for at least one of them to be found almost anywhere. Prairie onion (*A. stellatum*) likes rocky slopes and of course prairies; wild onion (*A. drummondii*) grows only on open prairies and plains; wild garlic (*A. canadense*) may be found almost anywhere the soil is rich and constantly moist, including open woods, marsh edges, and prairies; wild leek, the focus of this section, is found only in open hardwood forests.

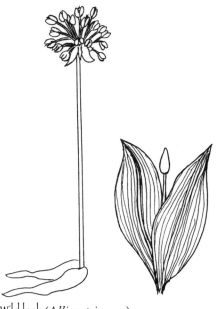

Wild leek (*Allium tricoccum*)

Although you probably wouldn't want to live on them exclusively, wild onions played an important part in the diet of precivilized America. The best-known example of this importance is the prairies at the southern end of Lake Michigan, a place the Ojibwa knew as She-Ka-Gon, or "Place of the Strong Onion Smell," and which has since become known as Chicago.

Smell is the key to identifying any member of the onion family, and the rule is that if it doesn't smell like an onion, throw it down and wash your hands before eating or handling food. Fly-poison (*Amianthium muscitoxicum*) is an exceptionally poisonous look-alike whose onionlike bulb was once crushed with sugar to attract and then kill houseflies that landed to feed. If you can't positively identify the species, but it smells like an onion, the worst you'll get is heartburn and bad breath. If it looks but doesn't smell like an onion, don't even consider eating it.

While most onions have long, thin, grasslike leaves, the wild leek is unique because of its paired spear-shaped spring leaves, which are probably an adaptation for gathering more light in its shaded growing environment. From late April to May the twin leaves grow in great profusion, covering damp forest floors with bright green foliage. By June these leaves have died and lie brown at the base of a long (6 to 18 inches) stalk with a ball-shaped cluster of white to pinkish star-shaped flowers at the top. In September the flowers fruit as purplish black berries, then the entire plant dies.

Leek bulbs are most tender and edible during the spring leafing stage, and grow stronger tasting as the season progresses. They are edible raw throughout the year, but in winter you'll probably want to limit their use to flavoring bland foods.

One very good and usually overlooked use for leeks and other wild onions is as an insect repellent. It's probably no coincidence that the vampires of Old World lore were repulsed by garlic, the family's most potent member, because the odor of onions also repels all types of bloodsucking insects. Crushing any part of an onion plant and applying the strongly scented juices to exposed skin constitutes one of the most effective insect repellents in nature. The odor also repels friends and loved ones, but it doesn't alarm animals because it's a natural scent, and if you're being eaten alive the choice is a no-brainer.

Watercress (*Nasturtium officinale*)

This single aquatic species of the mustard family is a truly global food plant, found in nearly every freshwater stream in the world. The irony is that watercress has always been a staple of supermodels and other professional dieters, who pay premium prices for this "exotic"

salad green—sometimes within sight of the waterways where it grows wild.

Like most wild vegetables, watercress is rich in vitamins A, C, and iron. It digests well in the human stomach, but perhaps its best feature is a sharp, horseradishlike taste (horseradish is also a mustard). The flavor is most pungent in raw plants, which add zest to any wild or cultivated salad, but if the plant is to be eaten as a main dish, boiling the greens for about 10 minutes greatly reduces their sharpness.

Watercress may be gathered and eaten at any time of

Watercress (*Nasturtium officinale*)

year. In summer it can be seen growing in sometimes profuse carpets of tangled vines, with spikes of tiny pollen-filled white to pink flowers rising above the water's surface from July through August. In snow country this evergreen plant is invaluable as a survival food, because it frequently grows in abundance and is the only living plant in the water during winter.

While watercress is itself safe to eat at any time, foragers should be aware that the plant is very hardy and will grow in waters polluted with pesticides or other toxins, absorbing these chemicals into its tissues. Avoid gathering the greens from any waterway that might be contaminated by runoff from crops, livestock, or golf courses. Heck, considering the outbreaks of flesh-eating fisteria those sources have already created, I'd avoid any waters they might drain into as well.

Be aware, too, that watercress vines are favored browsing places for aquatic snails that serve as intermediate hosts for numerous parasites dangerous to humans, *Giardia lamblia* being just one of them. Watercress meant to be eaten raw should be thoroughly washed first. Plants gathered as a potherb are completely safe if boiled for five minutes.

Violets (*Viola spp.*)

Violets are another of my favorite wild vegetables, largely because of their availability. There are more than 60 species in North America and more than 500 worldwide. I haven't tested all of them for edibility, but those I cover in this section are palatable, digestible, and common.

Violets are one of the first spring flowers to appear, and most bloom until midsummer with distinctive five-petaled flowers that always have one petal pointing downward. Depending

Common blue violet (*Viola sororia*)

on the species, flower colors may range from violet, like the common blue violet (*V. sororia*), to white, like the Canada violet (*V. canadensis*), to yellow, like the downy yellow violet (*V. pubescens*).

Colors notwithstanding, all three of these highly palatable wild vegetables fit the classic description of a violet. Leaves are heart shaped, dark green, and heavily veined with toothlike serrations around their perimeters. All of them prefer constantly moist soil—streambanks, lakeshores, dry swamps—and of course all have the unique five-petaled flowers, with two petals pointing upward, one to each side, and one petal pointing down.

Where you find one violet you'll probably find a bushel, a trait that I've found handy for feeding several people with "wilderness salad" during survival courses. The entire plant is edible, including the sugar-rich blossoms, but some folks have complained of diarrhea after eating a quantity of raw downy yellow violet. The common blue and Canada violets have never been implicated in digestive disorders; in any case, though, boiling removes the laxative quality.

Bracken Fern (*Pteridium aquilinum*)

Ferns are a common sight in forests, among rocks, and even in sand throughout North America, but few hikers spare them more than a passing glance, and fewer still realize how useful these humble plants could be if things suddenly went wrong.

Bracken is the most widespread and common of American ferns, found across the United States, southward into Mexico, and along the western coast of Canada northward to Alaska. It favors poor, sandy soils in open, moderately sunny forest, and is especially prevalent around pines.

In late April brackens first begin to appear as thick green shoots with distinctive curled-over tops, called fiddleheads because they resemble the ornate carvings around the tuning keys of a fine violin. The fiddleheads quickly grow into a fern 2 to 3 feet tall with lacy fronds that can exceed a foot in length, but bracken continues to sprout all summer, and its young shoots have considerable value as a wild vegetable. If the fiddlehead snaps off cleanly when you bend it—like a fresh green bean—it's just right for eating. Raw fiddleheads are entirely palatable but have a slimy core that I personally find objectionable.

Cooking them eliminates the sliminess, and they make an excellent dish by themselves or as a complement to other foods.

Beyond the fiddlehead stage, bracken stalks become woody, fibrous, and inedible, but the plant's usefulness goes on. Several layers of green fronds laid like shingles over a makeshift shelter frame makes as rainproof a roof as any natural material. A photography or hunting hide camouflaged with ferns

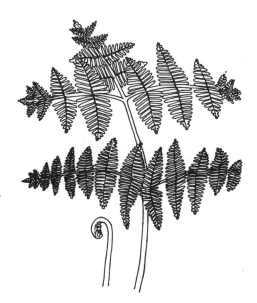

Bracken fern (*Pteridium aquilinum*)

in a field of ferns is virtually invisible from any distance. A pile of green ferns kept near a signal fire can be thrown onto the coals to produce an instant plume of thick white smoke above the forest canopy. In cold weather dead, dry ferns can be stuffed inside the sleeves and torso of a light jacket to create a layer of dead air that increases your warmth considerably. And as every woodsman of old knew well, a thick mattress of live or dead brackens is perhaps the warmest and most comfortable of natural beds.

A word of warning about gathering brackens: When the plant is mature, fibers in its tough stalk are sharp enough to painfully slice bare skin that slides along them. Anyone who has ever attempted to pull up brackens with his bare hands has lost some blood in the process. Always wear gloves when gathering mature ferns, or cut the stems with a sharp knife.

Broadleaf Cattail (*Typha latifolia*)

You can find cattails growing on every continent in every country that has a freshwater marsh, river, or lake, and where there are cattails a savvy woodsman can survive indefinitely. The long, vertical green leaves, sometimes more than 6 feet high, and distinctive cigar-shaped

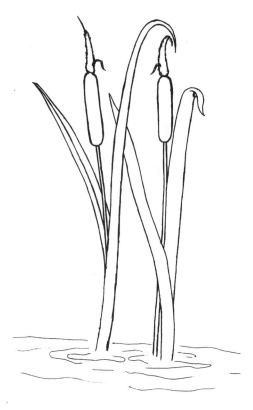

seedpods mounted atop arrow-straight stalks are unique among marsh plants.

Cattails are most important as a food source, and the common, or broadleaf, cattail and the narrowleaf cattail (*T. angustifolia*) are identical in this respect. Several parts of the plants are edible in season, but most classic survival manuals refer to the long taproot, which most liken to a potato. I wish it were so, but any similarity between a potato and a cattail root is limited to the fact that both contain starches that our bodies can efficiently convert to long-term energy. Cattail roots are tough with a hard woodlike core in any season, and the best method of

Broadleaf cattail (*Typha latifolia*)

preparing them as food is to boil them in lengths for 10 minutes then eat, swallowing what you can and spitting out the rest.

From spring to midsummer cattail shoots, plucked before they grow more than a foot tall, can be found in abundance, and they too contain starch and other nutrients. Once known as Russian asparagus, the shoots are gathered by pushing your first two fingers as deeply into the mud next to the plant's stalk as they can reach. Then, gripping the stalk close to the ground with your thumb, push the underground portion sideways with your fingers, snapping it off. This is much easier than trying to pull the tough plants up with sheer muscle. The snapped-off end will be creamy white and contains a crisp, celerylike core surrounded by tough, inedible layers. The tender cores, or cattail hearts, may be eaten raw by themselves (I like a bit of salt), or they can be boiled into other wilderness dishes.

Also considered edible by many survival experts are the green, cigar-shaped seedpods that top the plant's center stalk in midsummer. The typical instructions for their preparation include boiling for 10 minutes or so, then eating the immature seeds from around the stalk like corn on the cob. Personally, I find them to be like eating a saturated sponge, but they're probably nutritious enough.

The leaves of the cattail are not edible because they're too tough to digest, but the long fibers inside them can be fashioned into good makeshift rope, woven into sleeping mats and baskets, or used as camouflage.

Reindeer Moss (*Cladina rangiferina*)

When a team of Norwegian commandos parachuted into the mountains of their homeland to knock out a heavy-water plant that was key to Nazi A-bomb development in World War II, the entire operation went awry from the start. German soldiers spotted their parachutes during descent and set out in hot pursuit. The Germans were no match for Norwegians on skis, but the small unit was driven deep into the inhospitable winter Alps. There the commandos were forced to remain for three months with-

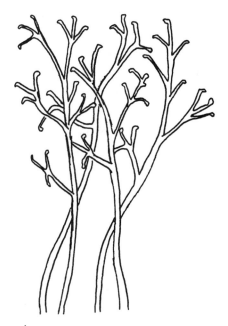

out resupply or respite from Nazi ski patrols, unable even to hunt for fear a gunshot would draw enemy attention. In the end, though, the little band of tough-as-nails Norwegians not only survived and eluded capture but in fact completed their mission and ruined Hitler's chances of beating America to the atomic bomb.

The reason those heroic men were in such good health after spending a hard winter under conditions that should have starved them

Reindeer moss (*Cladina rangiferina*)

can be attributed to one of nature's humblest life forms, a lichen known as reindeer moss. Like all members of this family, reindeer moss is a very primitive plant, half vegetable and half fungus. Reindeer moss is found on every continent and thrives on rock, sand, and acrid soils that will support few other plants.

Reindeer moss prefers open areas that get considerable sunshine, and it can best be described as irregularly shaped patches of subdued green, blue, and gray that resemble nothing so much as a thick shag carpet. In dry weather these clustered lichens crunch into powder underfoot, but they become spongy after soaking up dew or rain. When snow covers the ground, reindeer moss is still viable and edible, but of course it's harder to locate because you have to dig for it.

Nutritionally, reindeer moss is as complete a food as any in nature, but it wouldn't be my first choice as a steady diet. Eaten raw, the plants have a strong laxative effect that most folks would probably rather avoid, but the heat of cooking destroys this quality without harming their nutritional value. The most common cooking method is to boil a potful for five minutes, but lichen cakes—made with a flour of powdered dry lichens and water, then cooked on a flat rock like pancakes—have been used as survival food for millennia. Either method turns reindeer moss into a marginally palatable survival food, but most folks don't much care for the taste.

Reindeer moss is also known for its medicinal qualities, the most important of which is the broad-spectrum antibiotic it contains, even after cooking. Canadian sourdoughs also drink a tea made from reindeer moss, which is supposedly a mild stimulant, but drinking it creates an unpleasant burning sensation at the back of my throat.

An important nonfood use for reindeer moss is as a tinder material. The dry lichens can be lifted from the ground in chunks, and these are extremely flammable, igniting with just the touch of a match and burning hotly enough to start kindling.

Common Jewelweed (*Impatiens capensis*)

Jewelweed is also known as touch-me-not, which refers to the tendency of its delicate late-summer blossoms to fall off when touched. Another inspiration for the name is the plant's explosive fruits, which shoot seeds away from the parent with a coil spring that grows behind a seed until it bursts free of its hull. The plant is found throughout North America, from Texas to Alaska, and is abundant in almost any shaded, constantly moist forest or swamp.

Common jewelweed blooms from June through September and is easily identified then by its unique flowers, orange with black leopardlike spots and shaped like a horn of plenty. An otherwise identical subspecies, pale jewelweed (*I. pallida*), may be found in the same environment but has pale yellow flowers with no spots.

Jewelweed is also easy to identify when it isn't in bloom. The stalk, which may be

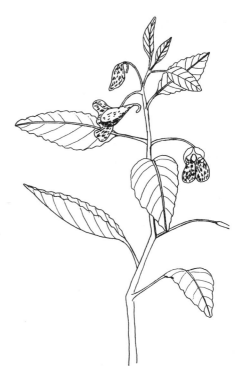

Jewelweed (*Impatiens capensis*)

upright on shorter plants but lying over on some that reach up to 8 feet, is pale green and succulent looking; it grows in disjointed segments, as if it had been broken in several places. The main stalk supports several branches along its length. Each branch supports several dark green, heavily veined leaves, spear shaped with serrated outer edges and growing in staggered pairs opposite one another. As is true with most plants in this section, where you find one jewelweed plant, you'll probably find a bunch of them.

Where you find jewelweed, you'll also find poison ivy, which is actually fortunate: The lotionlike juice of the jewelweed stalk today remains perhaps the best remedy ever found against poison ivy rash, and it's also one of the most effective fungicides against athlete's foot or jock itch. Simply crush the stalk in your hands and rub the juice from it directly onto the afflicted area, where it provides a soothing analgesic effect as well. Jewelweed juice is also good for heat and diaper rash, chafing, and even hives, but should not be taken internally. The plant isn't known to be toxic, but there's no value in eating it either.

Highbush Blackberry (*Rubus allegheniensis*)

While this familiar fruiting shrub is found primarily along open power lines, forest edges, and roadsides in the northeastern United States, I've had such good experience with it that it merits mention. Probably few people would fail to recognize the fat, sweet blackberry in season (September through October), but blackberry stalks are also well known for their sharp roselike thorns, which demand respect from passers-through. Leaves growing on each branch extending outward from the dark-colored main stalk are actually lobes, or parts of a single main leaf, growing outward on individual stems from a central location. These subleaves are spear shaped, rough, and heavily veined with serrated outer edges; they usually grow in groups of three or five, the latter of these arrayed in a distinctive star shape.

Medicinally, a stout tea made of shaved blackberry roots has proved invaluable to me on several occasions when survival students or companions had contracted a case of diarrhea. Diarrhea is a universal symptom of intestinal parasite infestation, but the cause is rarely so sinister among campers; most cases are attributable to a change in diet. Steeping two large, cut-up blackberry roots in a pint of boiling water yields a reddish sweet-smelling tea that has never failed to work to some degree, even against diarrhea caused by *Giardia*.

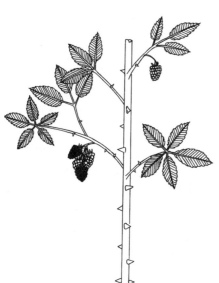

Blackberry (*Rubus allegheniensis*)

Sweet Joe-Pye Weed (*Eupatorium purpureum*)

While this common marsh plant isn't officially recognized as having medicinal value by the modern medical community, it belongs to a genus commonly known as bonesets, which Native Americans used in tea form to speed the knitting of broken bones. The fuzzy lavender flower heads are a common sight along wet riverbanks and shorelines from July through September. Sweet Joe-Pye weed grows throughout North America east of the Rockies; western Joe-Pye weed takes over west of the Rockies.

I haven't had occasion to use a boneset in its namesake capacity, but I have used sweet Joe-Pye weed, which is named for an Indian medicine man who used it extensively to treat various ailments, and was even credited with using it to stop a typhus epidemic. My own experience with the green, bitter-tasting tea made from Joe-Pye leaves has been limited to breaking fevers from colds, bronchitis, and influenza, and the results have been impressive. A cup of the awful-tasting stuff doctored with honey and lemon is generally sufficient to generate profuse sweating, followed by a break in the victim's fever. I don't know why it works, but it does.

Sweet Joe-Pye weed (*Eupatorium purpureum*)

Fragrant Cudweed (*Gnaphalium obtusifolium*)

No medicines have had more importance in elevating the health of humans and their animals in modern times than antibiotics, and fragrant cudweed, like the closely related pearly everlasting (*Anaphalis margaritacea*), is perhaps the most potent infection fighter in nature. That quality is said to have been discovered by early Old World cattle farmers, who noted that when sick cows threw up their cuds, feeding them this pleasant-smelling weed cured the stomach infection. Thus, the plant came to be known as cudweed.

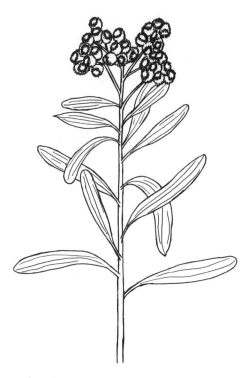

Cudweed (*Gnaphalium obtusifolium*)

I knew all of this for several years before actually trying it on myself during a flu epidemic in 1989. I steeped a strong tea from whole plants I'd gathered several months earlier, mixed in spearmint leaves and sugar to help kill its bitter taste, and forced down two mugfuls before retiring early. I awoke at 4:30 the following morning, possessed by an almost vibrant energy that demanded I get up and burn some of it off.

Though certain of my experience, I convinced five flu-stricken friends to try the same recipe, but didn't tell them about my own results. Three experienced overnight recoveries similar to mine, and the other two said they were feeling better. Since then cudweed has become a permanent staple of my family's home medicine chest. We've used it successfully against dental abscesses, tonsilitis and strep throat, sinus and ear infections, pinkeye, and inflamed stomach ulcers. Like any antibiotic, cudweed doesn't affect every germ that afflicts humans, but I personally think cudweed tea is far more effective overall than most prescription antibiotics.

For practical purposes there exists no real difference between the native pearly everlasting, found across North America from Alaska to Mexico, and the immigrant cudweed, which now grows almost everywhere east of the Rockies. Cudweed prefers open trails through swamp, sunny ditches, and other exposed places where the soil is rich and permanently moist. Pearly everlasting also likes open areas with lots of sun, but grows most abundantly in dry, sandy soil. Both contain the same antibiotic, and they have nearly identical leaves, flowers, and growth forms; neither is likely to be confused with any other plant in North America.

Cudweeds are best harvested in summer, when their bruised leaves emit a pleasantly distinctive odor. I've also had good results using dead standing plants gathered in midwinter, though they do seem less potent than those picked fresh. In his book *Using Plants for Healing*, noted horticultural writer Nelson Coon suggests a concentration of 1 teaspoonful of the powdered dried plant to 1 cup of boiling water. My own teas are generally a bit stronger, but I've never heard of anyone experiencing an adverse reaction to any dose.

Catnip (*Nepeta cataria*)

Probably everyone is familiar with this common plant's strange and apparently pleasant effect on felines, a phenomenon that has led some to call it cat marijuana. That intoxicating effect is caused by a poisonous oil in the leaves, excreted to repel plant-eating insects, and strong enough to actually kill bugs not repelled by odor alone.

Like so many useful plants, catnip isn't native, but was brought to North America from the Old World several centuries ago. And like so many of those immigrants, it has since escaped cultivation to become established throughout all but the northernmost regions of North America. The plants like rich, moist soil and a partially shaded environment, and are especially fond of wooded streambanks, ditches, and marsh edges.

Catnip (*Nepeta cataria*)

Catnip's most traditional use is as a bracing tea, which American colonists drank to settle upset stomachs, to relieve heartburn and nausea, and for its mildly stimulating effect. The recommended dose is an infusion (tea) of 1 ounce of dried, powdered plant per pint of boiling water.

But while many campers might enjoy a bracing cup of catnip tea, the reason I like catnip is because bugs of all types hate the odor of its juices. Crushing the entire plant by rolling it forcefully between your palms, then rubbing the wet pulp onto exposed skin, will discourage biting mosquitoes and blackflies for a half hour or more. Take care not to rub the oil into your eyes, though, because it can cause irritation.

Common Tansy (*Tanacetum vulgare*)

Like so many useful plants, this most commonly seen member of the tansy genus is actually a transplant, imported from the Old World as a spice herb, as a medicine, and for rituals. Today it can be found growing in moist open places across North America. Standing up to 5 feet tall, tansies typically grow in clusters of up to several hundred plants rooted close to one another. From July through October these plants are topped by clusters of small yellow dandelionlike flowers, but their frilly, spicy-smelling leaves and height make tansies easy to identify at almost any stage of growth.

Common tansy (*Tanacetum vulgare*)

In the days before grocery stores, powdered tansy tops—the most potent portion—were used as a pepper substitute, and some culinary books have included the leaves as a minor ingredient in salads. As a spice, tansy is okay, but I'm not going to leave the salt and pepper shakers out of my backpack.

But tansies are not food, and are in fact toxic if eaten in quantity. The upside of this is that sometimes the difference between poison and medicine lies in the dosage, and tansies have long been recognized as a potent remedy for intestinal parasites. A suggested treatment for *Giardia* and other parasitic worms is an infusion (tea) consisting of 1 ounce of fresh plant tops per pint of water, a cup of which is given to an otherwise fasting victim every morning and evening for two or three days.

Tansies were also used in ancient burial rites, not for any religious significance but because their spicy smell helped hide the odor of decaying flesh, while the toxins carried on the aroma worked to repel disease-carrying flies. Backpackers can appreciate both these qualities in places where biting bugs are a problem. Crush the entire plant into a ball and roll it between your palms until it becomes a wet mass, then rub these scented juices onto exposed skin. Crushed tansies can also be worn in a hatband or spread around a sleeping area to help keep the skeeterbugs at bay.

8

Survival

I t's tough to say precisely when folks who get along well with nature were branded collectively as lunatics, but the image currently conjured by Hollywood and the media is by and large about as accurate as their portrayal of doctors, lawyers, and cops. Rather than stigmatizing people who don't like the idea of dying from ignorance in the wild, the public might be better served by promoting the acquisition of wilderness survival skills.

In fact survival is more than just an activity; it's a way of life that most folks already practice in an environment other than the woods. Few would be foolish enough to set out on a long drive without a spare tire and the tools needed to change it, most households have at least some first-aid items, and almost no one sleeps without the constant vigilance of a smoke detector in the house. We take such precautions for the same reason a smart hiker carries compass, knife, and fire-starting kit: These tools are all safeguards that help keep common hazards from turning into major, even life-threatening problems.

McDougall's Laws of Wilderness Survival

1. The only monsters in the wilderness are those you brought with you.
2. Dry socks are far more important than clean underwear.
3. The southern sides of the tallest pines have the most branches.
4. Victims see what is; survivalists see what can be.
5. After 72 hours you'll be given up for dead.
6. The need for fire increases as conditions for starting one become more unfavorable.
7. Survival isn't a hobby, it's an attitude.
8. Hunting weapons can never substitute for hunting skills.
9. Your life has no value to nature.
10. The best remedy for any problem is to avoid it.
11. The quality of your equipment reflects the value you place on your own life.
12. If you can start a fire, you'll never freeze to death.
13. Humans have no sense of direction.
14. You're your own best bet for staying well in the wilderness.
15. If it's nontoxic, digestible, and palatable, it's food.
16. The most dangerous animals in the woods have six legs.
17. The easy way is generally smartest.
18. Animals have teeth and claws for the same reasons humans must carry a knife.
19. In the Northern Hemisphere the sun always travels east to west in the southern sky.
20. No human is too tough to get broken.
21. Every human is tough enough to survive.

Shelter

In foul weather, shelter may be the most pressing survival need. Where I live death from hypothermia can and has occurred in every season, and the most dangerous conditions I've experienced came not during subzero blizzards but from prolonged exposure to even warm rain. Hikers know that saturating their canteen covers with water serves to keep the liquid inside about 20 degrees Fahrenheit cooler than the ambient temperature. The same truth applies to hikers themselves. Throw in a stiff wind with its evaporative cooling effect and a 70-degree day can turn cold enough to kill. Savvy hikers guard against these dangers with extra clothing in a day pack, but the best defense against a cold rain, wet snow, or freezing wind is to find shelter.

Modern lightweight bivy shelters are an option, but a 10-foot-square sheet of ordinary verathane (plastic), like those used as drop cloths by painters, serves very well in any weather. Priced at $2 or less and weighing just a few ounces, depending on mil thickness, a plastic drop cloth can be suspended from a cord tied between two trees to form a pup tent, or draped over a simple wooden frame to make a weather-proof shelter. If you already have a tent or bivy, the drop cloth can serve as a spare rainfly, as a tarpaulin for covering your backpack, or as an impromptu awning while fishing a favorite trout hole in the rain.

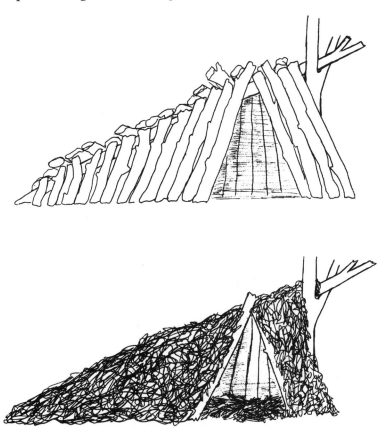

The debris hut relies on all-natural materials for insulated warmth.

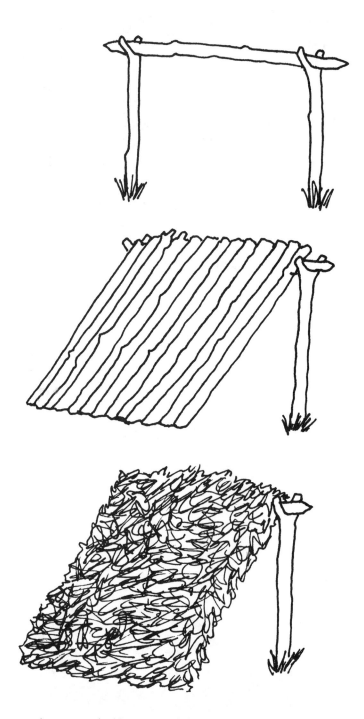

A lean-to is also a way to build your own shelter. Its quick and easy to erect, but should only be used as a mild weather shelter, not for long term.

An above-ground view of an earth dugout shelter.

Repairing tears or holes in the field is as simple as covering them with a strip of sticky vinyl (electrical) tape.

In situations where you might be forced to ground for several days by foul weather, a frame-type shelter offers better protection and comfort during long hours—or days—of howling winds, whipping snow, or pounding rain than a plastic pup tent. The emergency shelter I recommend most often for such times is the debris hut, so called because it employs existing wood, leaves, and other dead, natural debris in its

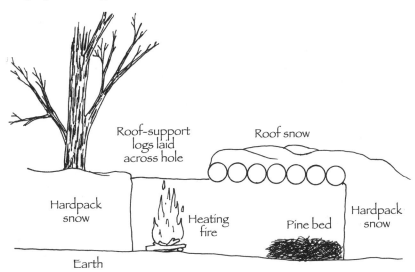

Properly built, the below-ground shelter known as the snow dugout enables hikers to weather even the most extreme temperatures and conditions.

composition. Nearly every environment provides materials sufficient for its construction, and a debris hut is easily sealed off to weather the fiercest storm. A plastic drop cloth draped over the shelter's frame and held in place by the weight of branches leaned against its side makes for a dry, snug place to wait out thunderstorms. Once I even spent an unplanned day in a low, one-man debris hut while a snowstorm with -50 windchills blew by.

In places that have 4 or 5 feet of hardpack snow, the shelter I most recommend is the snow dugout. Put simply, this is a hole about 7 feet in diameter, extending downward from the snow's surface to bare ground, and most easily created by the heat of a blazing fire. Form a roof by laying long sticks and branches side by side across one half of the hole, and then packing on a foot or so of insulating snow to seal out drafts. Lay a bed of wood under the roof and pad it with pine boughs, ferns, or grass to keep your body heat from being absorbed by damp earth during sleep.

The open, uncovered half of the hole contains a heating and cooking fire, which, because it's below ground level, is unaffected by wind. Heat thrown by the fire is radiated from all around by the dugout's vertical snow walls, and any windchill effect is completely negated. I comfortably weathered a three-day blizzard in a snow dugout in 1984, and when I finally emerged on a clear, sunny day, I found that local authorities had written me off for dead.

Fire

"If you can start and maintain a fire, you'll never freeze to death." This wilderness truism should be taken to heart by every camper in every season anywhere in North America. Fire makes it possible to cook foods and boil water to kill parasites, it gives an injured camper one of the most effective means yet discovered of signaling for help, and the crackling of a hot fire on a cold night warms both the body and spirit.

But the art of making fire—second nature to every kid old enough to learn it a few generations ago—has become unnecessary in a world of self-lighting ranges, butane lighters, gas grills, and forced-air heat. I've often slyly observed campers at state parks while they tried in vain to light piles of wood afire with paper, Styrofoam, dry leaves, whole books of matches, and anything else that looked combustible. Most are men, of course, because making fire is after all a hairy man's job. I'd never offer advice in that testosterone-charged atmosphere of urban man battling the forces of nature, but many a wife and girlfriend has prompted spectacular arguments by making suggestions.

As a hiker or backpacker, you can't afford the luxury of fooling around with a campfire, and the times when you'll need a fire the most are most likely to be in heavy rain, wind, snow, and other conditions that don't favor its creation. Regardless of the weather, you can start a fire, but only if you follow proper fire-building protocol.

Build is the operative word when making fire. The most common mistake I've seen is trying to force a campfire from wood to crackling blaze in one step. It doesn't work that way. Building a fire is something like

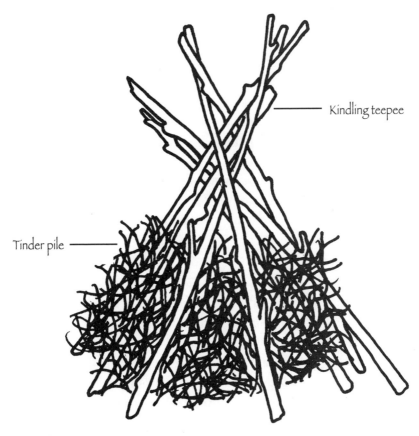

Kindling teepee

Tinder pile

Building a campfire is a delicate and methodical process that demands both patience and diligence.

raising kids (only faster): You start with a tiny spark of life, then coax and feed it in careful, gentle steps until it becomes self-sustaining. Push it too fast and a flame will smother; neglect it and the spark will starve to death.

To start, you must have the four components of a campfire: a temporary heat source, highly combustible tinder, hot-burning kindling, and, finally, heavy slow-burning fuel. The first of these can range from a Blast Match fire starter (see chapter 1) to the time-honored trick of using a lighted candle in wet weather—anything that produces sufficient heat of sufficient duration to ignite available tinder. Chemical tinder cubes, along with trioxane and hexamine bars, guarantee the first self-sustaining stage of a campfire in any weather, but in most cases dry natural materials like grass, pine needles, reindeer moss, birch bark, and pine sap burn at the touch of a flame.

The next step is to slowly feed the flaming pile of tinder material with kindling. This begins as a delicate process in which the burning tinder is gently covered by a tepee of the smallest, driest twigs available, none larger in diameter than a pencil. The tepee configuration permits maximum heat transference to the outer surfaces of the kindling, until it too ignites and begins feeding on itself. When the first layer of tiny kindling produces a plume of flame, slowly add progressively larger twigs until the fire is strong enough to burn any wood thrown on it. If you're gathering kindling in the rain, dead, barkless twigs still attached to the parent tree or shrub will be the driest, because rain runs off them; sticks lying on the ground absorb more water.

The Coal Bed

One of the most vital yet overlooked components of real-life survival is the ability to get at least five hours of sound, restful sleep each night. Even in warm climates nighttime chills and heavy dewfalls can induce mild to severe hypothermia, and it's tough to get a good night's sleep when your body is shivering violently. Lack of proper sleep can sap the body's immune system literally overnight, allowing infections to gain a foothold. Throw in cold or wet conditions and you have the same scenario that used to terrify our forebears when pneumonia was almost always a fatal disease.

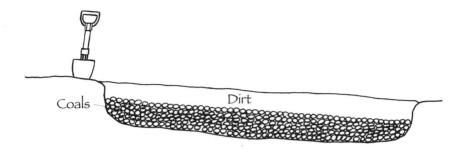

The coal bed

The coal bed is a time-honored and potentially lifesaving trick that woodsmen of old knew well and used often to supplement their horse-blanket bedrolls. Like all the best survival techniques, the coal bed is simple to understand and employ. It consists of a body-length depression at least 6 inches deep (more is better), the bottom of which has been lined with about 3 inches of fresh, red-hot coals. Loose soil taken from the excavation is used to re-cover the live coals to a tamped depth of at least 4 inches, well away from a sleeper's body. Cover the dirt with a mat of small live evergreen twigs, green ferns, or green cattail leaves to help keep the soil in place as you roll in your sleep. Finally, cover the whole thing with a groundsheet if one is available, and turn into your bedroll for a night of sound sleep, awakening rested and ready to tackle whatever comes in the morning. Lying on soil that doesn't actively absorb body heat is a great advantage by itself, but a coal bed will continue to generate noticeable heat long after a sleeper rises—about 10 hours in my experience.

Modern ultralight backpackers might also appreciate that a small bivy or tent set atop a completed coal bed will allow the most minimalist summer backpacker to withstand any freak cold snaps down to and below the 0 mark. If you have no equipment at all, lie on the bed and cover yourself with a large, deep pile of dead leaves, bracken ferns, sand, or even dirt. The only danger, which I must repeat a warning against, is not placing enough insulating dirt atop the coals.

Water

Historical novels have often referred to the North America of old as a pristine wilderness with waters so sweet and pure that a buckskin-clad frontiersman could slake his thirst from any of them with impunity. That romantic notion is every bit as dangerous now as it was when whole settlements, ignorant of the dangers or even the existence of microbes and parasites, were wiped out by waterborne diseases.

In fact no natural water anywhere on earth has ever been above suspicion. In the United States alone 25 percent of doctor-diagnosed cases of diarrhea are attributed to *Giardia lamblia,* a very common and occasionally fatal parasitic intestinal worm. Otherwise healthy victims usually suffer a week or so of painful, debilitating cramps and dehydrating bowel movements, and expel the parasites naturally within one to two months. But victims with an already depressed immune system typically require medical treatment, and a few have died after their symptoms were misdiagnosed as stomach flu. Discovered in the 19th century, *Giardia* wasn't recognized as a pathogen capable of infecting humans until 1981, when hikers began contracting it from clear Rocky Mountain streams.

The unpleasant truth is that giardiasis and many other waterborne diseases, including deadly ones like cholera and typhoid, are almost always transmitted through ingestion of untreated water contaminated by feces. Excepting beavers, which are blamed for *Giardia* transmission (known to trappers of old as beaver fever), animals are generally careful not to contaminate their own drinking supply with feces. This instinctive revulsion to its own scat appears to be more pronounced the more susceptible a species is to parasitic infections.

But eggs of trematodes—a diverse family of aquatic parasitic worms that infest humans, and of which *Giardia lamblia* is just one member—do find their way into water from the scat deposits of parent hosts. On reaching water an egg typically hatches into a free-swimming microscopic miracidium, which actively seeks out an intermediate host. This host is most often a snail, but some trematodes also infect fish and crayfish.

The miracidium burrows into its host's flesh, drawing sustenance while it metamorphoses first into a sporocyst. Each sporocyst serves as an incubation chamber for several rediae, which themselves contain several cercariae. From there, the free-swimming mature cercariae escape the intermediate host and, in most cases, mature into flukes that are ingested by the secondary, usually final, host. Once inside this parent host, flukes move to the intestines (*Giardia*), liver, lungs, or whatever organ the particular species infests, and develop into adults, feeding on their victims while eggs develop inside them. Dead adults and viable eggs are expelled in feces, washed back into the water by rain and snowmelt, and the process begins anew.

Sanitation

Homo sapiens is susceptible to a wide variety of waterborne diseases, and we have the most foul excreta, in terms of posing health hazards, of any creature on earth. Taking a cue from animals, campers should always answer the call of nature a minimum of 100 feet from any source of water, including natural springs and other runoffs.

The most effective means of dealing with excreta is burial under whatever medium is available. Of primary concern is isolating it from disease-carrying flies that might spread contamination, but burial also accelerates decomposition, shortening the transition time between toxic waste and rich soil.

On the trail a simple slit trench excavated with a boot heel or another digging tool in soft soil is usually adequate. It needn't be deep, because few wild animals are likely to investigate such strong human spoor, but should be covered completely afterward. For this same reason, folks out to find wild animals should take the added precaution of sealing the re-covered trench with a dead log or large stone to further reduce odors.

In a wilderness camp, especially one where several people will be spending a day or more, digging a more elaborate and deeper slit-trench latrine should be high on the list of things to do right after dropping your packs. Natural foliage, perhaps aided by a groundsheet tied between trees, helps ensure privacy, but the goal is to keep waste matter confined at least 100 feet from camp (again, farther is better) to avoid possible contamination by flies. The trench should be at least 2 feet deep by 1 foot wide by about 3 feet long, with loose soil piled to one side for use in covering each new deposit. Just fill in the trench completely prior to leaving; nature does the rest.

Purification

For filling canteens and water bottles, natural springheads that flow directly from a hillside have always proved safe to drink untreated, but no other water source can ever be considered safe, regardless of how clean it might appear. Since you can't tell visually if a body of water is contaminated, the best plan is to purify all water drawn from any source.

The oldest and best-known method of purifying water is to boil it for five minutes. For altitudes above 2,000 feet, increase that time to seven minutes to compensate for lower atmospheric pressure. At sea level water boils at 212 degrees Fahrenheit, but higher elevations can lower the boiling point considerably. Covering a boiling pot with a loose lid raises the pressure against the water, forcing it to reach higher temperatures before boiling and lessening evaporation loss.

The second best-known purification method is to treat raw water chemically with iodine tablets or three drops of liquid iodine antiseptic per quart. I've included a bottle of iodine in my wilderness kit for decades, but while no one I know has ever contracted anything from drinking water treated with it, recent tests have shown that the cryptosporidium, another dangerous parasite, may be resistant to iodine. Aside from this, iodized water has a taste that makes drinking it only slightly preferable to being thirsty, so I generally doctor it with Kool-Aid.

With either of the above techniques, it will at some point become necessary to filter the sediment from drinking water before you treat it. Safe or not, few can swallow gritty, murky water without gagging, so I always carry a large handkerchief (a "dog-rag" to Vietnam vets) to pour water through from one vessel into another. Note that straining water through cloth does nothing to make it safe to drink, but only removes sediment and larger aquatic bugs.

The most recent and best water purifier is the modern pump-type microfilter. I currently own two, a SweetWater Guardian+Plus and a Voyageur from Pur, and one of them is with me whenever I'm in the woods, even on short hikes. These units and others like them work by using a pump to force raw water under great pressure through a porous microfilter that removes virtually all parasitic organisms and bacteria. Both units also remove most toxic chemicals, like herbicides, pesticides, and fertilizer washed away from farmlands and golf courses, something neither boiling nor iodine can do.

The condensation still, however, removes everything but water. This very effective water purification tool has special importance to folks driving the backcountry in a 4x4 or ATV, because they generally have the gas can, hose, and tools needed to make one on board. If you have the necessary components, the rest is child's play.

In principle the condensation still does nothing more than funnel water heated to steam inside a closed environment through a hose that serves as its only escape. Inside the hose steam vapors cool, recombine, and condense into distilled water, having left whatever contaminants they once contained inside the heating vessel. Small gasoline cans with hoses already attached to their tops are almost custom made for use as a condensation still, but remember that the output can only be as safe as the hose it ran through. Never fill the can you use more than half full of untreated water, and never apply more than a small fire to its base. Output from a condensation still can exceed a dozen gallons of pure water per day from any salt- or fresh-water source.

Water bottles are largely a matter of preference, and my own is the GI plastic 1-quart canteen with canvas or nylon cover and steel cup. This multifunctional unit attaches securely to any belt or strap with ALICE clips, carries comfortably, and serves well as a field mess or water purification kit. Water can be boiled in the canteen cup, then poured into the canteen after cooling. Saturating the padded cover with water

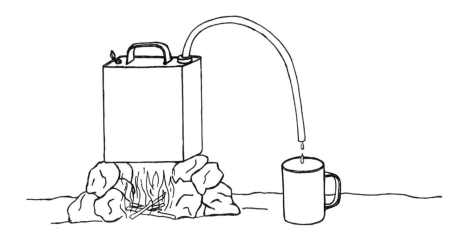

A small gasoline-type can with a hose attached easily transforms into a condensation still. Just add fire and water.

provides an evaporative cooling effect that keeps water in the canteen about 20 degrees Fahrenheit cooler than the air.

Most important, understand that *Giardia lamblia, Schistosoma japonicum, Opisthorchis felineus,* and a host of other parasites and bugs that infest man may be present in any natural water. Few are lethal, because it's not in a parasite's best interest to kill its host, but none is pleasant, and all are to be avoided. Not long ago one of my backpacking companions foolishly tested his immunity by drinking directly from a clear river in Michigan's Upper Peninsula; he spent the last two days of a four-day trip in camp with nausea, diarrhea, chills, and fever. My friend recovered, but he can tell you with more conviction than I that some lessons are best not learned through experience.

Food

My survival courses focus heavily on finding natural foods that are palatable, nutritious, and digestible. I don't care that wilderness survival dogma maintains that food is unimportant because it takes a human three months to starve. I've seen and experienced the unpleasant way low blood-sugar levels cause an active hiker to suffer a kind of trauma as his hungry body begins hoarding resources. The result is general fatigue, clumsiness, and impaired judgment, any of which could prove dangerous.

A number of wild plants that meet the criteria for food are described in chapter 7, but don't overlook unconventional sources of energy. I make it a point to eat grubs in my survival classes, because these socially repulsive insect larvae are especially high in readily usable proteins and essential fats, and generally abundant in rotting wood everywhere. They're best cooked to prevent any possibility of contracting a parasite, and if you can't bring yourself to chew, it's okay to swallow the easily digested animals whole.

Snakes of any species are edible and tasty, and even venomous species pose no challenge to a person armed with a long stick: A hard blow to the head kills it. Be very careful, though, to immediately remove and discard the heads of rattlesnakes, which have been known to bite reflexively more than an hour after being separated from their bodies. A slit from belly to anus allows entrails to be pulled out cleanly, after which it's just a matter of stripping off the skin in a single piece, then cooking the remaining meat and bones by whatever means are available.

Ants, too, are an abundant source of nutrition. All species have a high content of natural sugars in their bodies, and formic acid gives them a not-unpleasant sour taste. The problem of getting enough of the tiny critters to make a meal is solved by taking a lesson from chimpanzees, which knock off an anthill's top, then insert a twig into the mass of crazed insects. But instead of licking the insects off the twig like a chimp, I brush them into a cooking pot and crush them. Roasting the dead ants over a fire until dry, then crushing again, results in a sweetish powder that can be mixed with water and baked into "ant cookies," added to other foods, or eaten as is.

Frogs have always been a valuable source of food for me personally, partly because I like frog legs, but in large part because frogs are such easy, abundant prey. With a stout, 5-foot stick in hand, simply walk slowly along the shoreline of ponds and other wet places populated by frogs. Although well camouflaged, most will jump into the water at your approach, then immediately stick their heads up to see what's going on. At this point I smack the frog hard with my stick and pick up my dead floating prize. All frogs are edible, but if the only species available are small, remove the entrails, feet, and head, peel off the skin, and cook the entire frog to get as much meat from it as possible.

Survival Knots

Few skills have served me so well or so often as the ability to tie a small variety of basic knots—for lashing together emergency snowshoes or a survival shelter, for tying fishing lines and snares, and for just fastening all sorts of things together in some manner.

Rock climbers can probably ignore or even add to this section, but every outdoorsman of either sex and any discipline in every season should have a working knowledge of working knots.

I'd like to preface this section with a recommendation that every hiker carry at least 20 feet of stout nylon cord. I know how to make rope from plant fibers—I keep 20 feet of ½-inch cattail rope around to impress greenhorns, and I teach rope making in my survival classes—but nature doesn't provide anything to equal the strength and rot resistance of nylon cord.

Square Knot

The square knot is used when you want to fasten together two loose ends of a rope or ropes. It's a fast, simple knot that unties easily by feel, but holds tight with the strength of whatever it's tied with. This is the

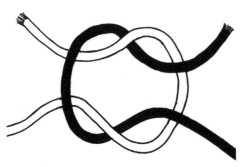

knot I use most often in daily life, even to tie my shoes (they never come untied in rough country), and the first knot every hiker should learn to tie in the dark.

To tie a square knot, follow these steps: With a rope end in each hand, cross the right end over the left to form

Square knot

an X, with the right rope on top of the left. Wrap the right rope end, which is now on the left, down around the left rope, then back upward, making one complete turn around the left rope. Next, cross the two ends again, with the left end over the right end; wrap the right end, which is now on the left, over the left end; and pull both ends apart, which pulls the finished square knot tight.

Double Half-Hitch Slipknot

Also important is knowing how to tie a double half hitch, the sliding slipknot used for snares and other applications where a loop that closes tighter the harder it's pulled against is needed. This knot is tied by taking one end of a cord and forming it into a circle by crossing the free end behind, then wrapping the free end once around the circle, bringing it parallel with the main length of cord leading to the loop. Next, wrap the free end

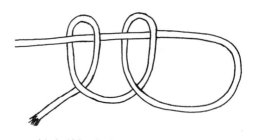

Double half-hitch slipknot

around behind the main length, then back through the loop formed by that step. Pull the free end tight and you have a sliding noose that will only draw tighter around whatever it's tied to when pulled against.

Timber Hitch Knot

The timber hitch is a simple variation of the double half hitch that gets its name from loggers, who once used it to drag out large trunks with horses. A slipknot noose tends to slide lengthwise along whatever it's tied to when pull is applied parallel to the object, so timbermen "locked" the knot with another loose half hitch wrapped around the log and back through itself. Although not stable enough to pull against by itself, the slipknot offers sufficient resistance to pull the half hitch above it tight with a vise-like grip that won't slide. A more camping-oriented use of the timber hitch is for securing a hammock between two smooth-trunked trees.

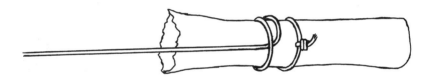

Timber hitch knot

Bowline Knot

A bowline is the knot that search-and-rescue folks use to tie nonsliding loops that a rescuee can place under his arms or step into during an air rescue. Boaters find it useful for tying permanent, loose loops in bowlines, which can be quickly thrown over a piling when docking in rough water. As the accompanying illustration shows, the bowline knot is essentially a trio of interlocking loops, each of which constricts more tightly around the next when pull is applied.

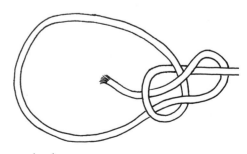

Bowline knot

Fisherman's Knot

The last knot you really need to know is the fisherman's knot, a self-tightening slipknot used to tie slippery monofilament fishing line to hooks and swivels, and the only knot that can be depended upon to hold that greasy-slick stuff. The first step is to run about 6 inches of line through or around the object you're tying to, then wrap the free end around the line in eight (traditional) snug turns, back through the loop formed at the bottom, then through the loop formed by that action. Pull the free end with a firm sawing motion to tighten the knot and you're ready to fish.

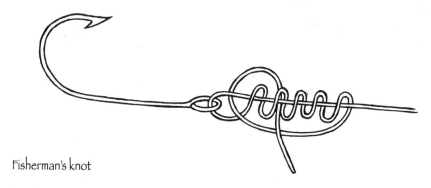

Fisherman's knot

Survival Skills

While almost everything in this book falls into the category of survival skills in one way or another, the projects I've selected for this section represent important, perhaps lifesaving techniques that can be employed using the tools at hand. I recommend learning all of them, but even more strongly, I urge you to be prepared with modern tools that make using these skills unnecessary.

Snowshoes

I have a demonstrated knack for learning things the hard way, and one of these lessons was that deep snow can effectively strand a camper, hiker, or snowmobiler who doesn't have snowshoes. In my own case an unseasonable warm spell forced me to break camp and pack out at 3:30 A.M., when the waist-deep hardpack was frozen solid. I knew that with sunrise the hardpack would become too soft to support my weight, making every step a bone-jarring, exhausting effort. I made the 10-mile

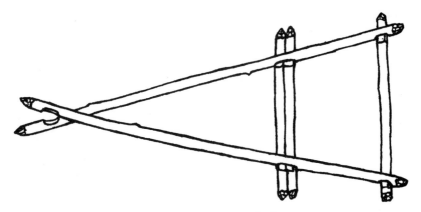

Making emergency snowshoes: Wood pieces are notched (a),

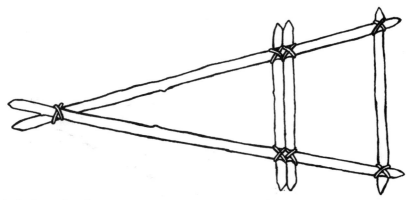

lashed together (b),

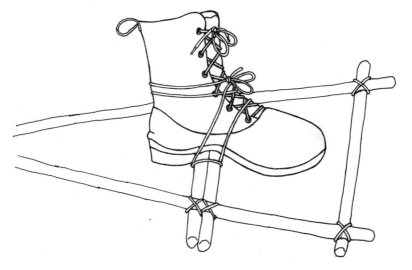

and strapped to the foot (c) as shown.

trip back to town okay, but folks in similar circumstances have died within just a few miles of civilization.

Not long after this experience I learned to fashion emergency snowshoes, and I'll never again be stranded by snow. To make them, you'll need a sturdy belt knife and eight or ten more or less straight lengths of green wood least an inch in diameter (four or five pieces per shoe). The frame of the shoe is essentially an elongated triangle, with the base formed by a foot-long crosspiece lashed across the ends of two 3-foot lengths. The heel, or pointed end of the frame, is made by lashing the free ends of the longer pieces together. Whittle notches halfway through each piece where it joins with another to help lock the component lengths more tightly when they're lashed in place.

The last and most critical part of an emergency snowshoe is the arch crosspiece (or crosspieces, as in the illustration), the piece your foot will be on while walking. It must be positioned to span the longer lengths of the frame at a point where the tail (pointed) end is heaviest and swivels downward when the shoe is raised, but far enough from the front crosspiece to allow clearance between itself and your boot toes. It's important that the tail of each shoe drags, or "tracks," when you raise your foot to take a step, because tracking helps keep the shoe from twisting underfoot while raising the front upward to avoid tripping hazards. When you've determined the best location for the arch crosspiece(s), notch the intersections and lash them tightly together.

The final step is to fasten the snowshoes to your feet and walk home. With boot heel pressed against the arch crosspiece(s), lay the center of a 2-foot length of cord across your instep, wrap the ends under the crosspiece(s), then cross the ends over your instep, around the ankle, and tie them as you would a shoe. There may be a tendency for the snowshoes to slip sideways while walking, and if this becomes a problem you can fix it by cutting shallow grooves in the arch crosspiece(s) on each side of your boots to help anchor the binding cord.

Bow-and-Drill Fire Starter

The bow-and-drill fire starter has been giving humans the means to keep warm, cook, and repel animals since before recorded history. Construction and operation are simple, but mastery requires considerable practice, and while everyone should be familiar with the bow-and-drill,

I very much recommend taking precautions to ensure you never need to use this last-ditch fire starter.

The bow part of the tool is what its name implies, a length of cord tied to each end of a springy green stick about 2 feet long by ½ inch in diameter. The string should be taut, but not so tight that it bends the bow.

The drill is a smooth, straight length of dry wood, 8 to 10 inches long by about 1 inch in diameter. One end is whittled to a dull point, the other rounded off. Also true to its name, the drill is intended to spin quickly, so it's important that it be as straight as possible to prevent unnecessary wobble and wasted energy.

To hold the top of the drill in place as it spins you need a handle, essentially a palm-size piece of flat, dry wood with a shallow hole in its center that accommodates the top, rounded end of the drill. Start by drilling out the hole with your survival knife until the end of the drill fits into it, then add some sand and spin the two components forcefully against one another to achieve an ideal fit.

The last piece in a bow-and-drill outfit is the fireboard, a more or less flat slab of dry wood against which the pointed end of the drill spins with enough friction to cause combustion. The best source for fireboards in any wooded environment will be rotting stumps and logs, the outer layers of which remain hard long after the softer cores have turned to powder. The ideal fireboard need not be more than 6 inches wide, but it should be at least 2 feet long because you'll be holding it in place with one foot while sawing the drill against it.

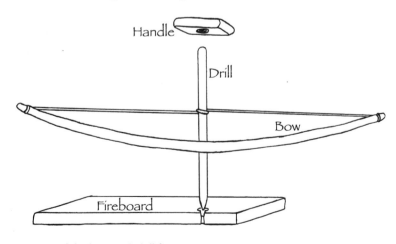

Components of the bow-and-drill fire starter

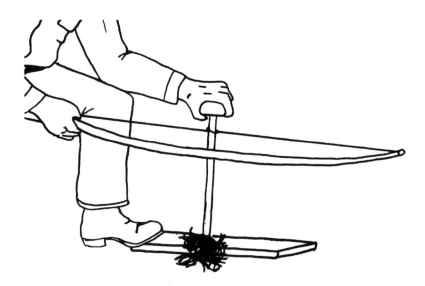

Using a bow-and-drill to start a fire can be frustrating for beginners—but practiced hands make short work of it.

Another reason for this length is to allow the creation of several fire notches along each side of the fireboard. Each notch begins as a V-shaped cut in the board's outer edge, about ½ inch wide and equally deep. A shallow hole drilled at the V's point accommodates the pointed end of the drill.

To use the bow-and-drill (assuming you're right-handed), wrap the bowstring one turn around the drill, place your left foot on the fireboard, and place your right knee on the ground. Place a pile of easily lighted tinder, like dry grass or powdered reindeer moss, under the fireboard notch you'll be using. Insert the pointed end of the drill into its mating hole in the fireboard, and hold it in place by inserting the rounded end into the handle hole and pressing lightly downward with your left hand. With left elbow resting on your left knee and the bow in your right hand, begin sawing the bow back and forth, causing the drill wrapped in its string to spin. Gently, smoothly, and continuously sawing the bow back and forth (that's the hard part) causes friction between fireboard and drill, and soon a plume of smoke will rise from it. The next phase is char, a hot, dark brown wood powder that becomes hotter and darker as you continue working the bow (is your arm tired yet?), finally igniting into a small glow of smoldering life atop the dry tinder pile.

When the tinder pile begins to emit a steady plume of smoke, remove the fireboard and very gently blow the spark into a flame. Immediately add more tinder and tiny dry sticks to keep the flame going until it can sustain itself, and build it into a campfire.

Using a bow-and-drill is frustrating and strenuous for beginners, but here are a few tricks that make coaxing fire out of it a bit easier: Add a little dry sand to the fireboard hole to increase friction between it and the drill. Drip wax from a lighted candle into the drill cavity in the handle to create a more slippery bearing surface between the two. Coat the bowstring with pine sap to give it better traction against the drill body. Beyond these, my only advice is to practice.

Setting Snares

The spring snare is a topic that intrigues most outdoorsmen, judging from the number of questions I field on the subject, and most are surprised at how simple these devices are to construct. In principle a force sufficient to kill its victim—usually supplied by a bent sapling—is restrained by a trigger, which is itself tenuously connected and requires only a slight bump to disengage, releasing the pent-up spring force. After this it's mostly a matter of deciding where to place the noose.

The simplest and most effective spring snare is a version known as the pencil snare, so called because it uses a long, narrow stick—the pencil—as its trigger. The pencil is attached by the snare cord to the spring, and held in place under pressure by a pair of notched stakes driven into the ground on each side of a game trail. With the ends of the pencil set as precariously as possible in the stake notches and a loose slipknot noose hanging below across an animal trail, all that remains is for a victim to come along. When it does, ideally the animal's head will pass through the noose, which catches against its shoulders and begins to tighten. This sends the animal into a panic, whereupon it tries to flee, pulling against the pencil, which slips free of the stakes, releasing the spring and yanking the hapless victim aloft.

Be warned, however, that few snares yield results, because more important than how well you set them is knowing the animal for which they're set. This, unfortunately, means that the effectiveness of a snare or any other trap set is largely dependent on experience. Practice setting the pencil snare until you're familiar with its workings, and if you must

The pencil snare, like any snare, should never be set unnecessarily or left unattended.

employ snares in a real-life survival scenario, set as many as you can to boost chances for success. But please, never set snares unnecessarily or leave them set unattended.

Emergency Signals

I frequently use one of the internationally recognized emergency ground-to-air signals shown on the accompanying table (see page 154), the LL pattern. I know that this signal means "I'm okay," but it's one of those ironies in life that the more humans carve up the wilderness with roads and trails, the more search-and-rescue types come out to see if I'm all right. It's getting so I have to file an itinerary with local authorities to avoid being rescued.

But it's nice to know that these folks are around, just in case. Since most of a search is typically conducted from the air, it pays to know the same set of ground-to-air signals that SAR pilots are taught to recognize. Symbols can be formed on the ground by several means, from laying them out with pieces of deadwood, to stamping them into the snow, to forming them (carefully) with a bed of flaming coals for the nighttime. In all cases the signals should of course be laid out in an open place, be large enough to be obvious from several hundred feet above, and contrast as much as possible with the surrounding earth.

Fire and smoke are also effective means of getting attention from both ground and air. During daylight wet, rotting wood thrown onto a bed of hot coals produces a thick plume of white smoke. At night a tall tepee of long dry sticks built over a small campfire will quickly flame up into a beacon that can be seen from several miles, but always anticipate that the flaming tepee will fall over as it burns down, and take precautions.

Not many lost hikers signal for help with signal mirrors. This is a statistically established fact that has been repeated by several search-and-rescue authorities. But rather than demonstrating a low opinion of signal mirrors and their effectiveness, that assertion actually reveals how few travelers in the backcountry take advantage of this useful survival tool.

Having packed a number of signal mirrors over the years, I've now settled on just one, the Star Flash mirror from Survival, Inc. (see the source list on page 52), currently standard issue for U.S. Air Force and space shuttle survival kits. This mirror measures 2 by 3 inches, weighs less than an ounce, and features a clear, undistorted reflective surface those old stainless-steel jobs never had. The mirror body is composed of tough Lexan polycarbonate molded from each side to form a hollow airtight center that makes this mirror float on water—another first. A molded lanyard hole in one corner allows the Star Flash to be worn around the neck. Retail is $6 at most outfitters.

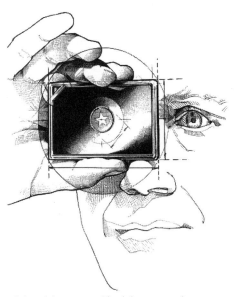

While seldom carried by hikers, signal mirrors, like this Star Flash model by Survival, Inc., have proven to be a useful survival tool. *Courtesy Survival, Inc.*

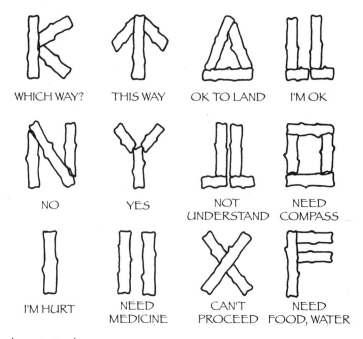

WHICH WAY?	THIS WAY	OK TO LAND	I'M OK
NO	YES	NOT UNDERSTAND	NEED COMPASS
I'M HURT	NEED MEDICINE	CAN'T PROCEED	NEED FOOD, WATER

Ground-to-air signals

All signal mirrors have a sighting hole in their centers, sometimes in a cross shape, sometimes in a star. Its purpose is to help you aim reflected light without blinding you with direct sunlight. With the sighting hole to one eye and your opposite eye closed, locate the target (most likely an airplane) in the sight. Move the mirror back and forth, up and down, until a red spot appears on the target, telling you that light is being reflected directly at it. After this signals can be sent by flashing the target, or you might opt to just keep a steady stream of sunlight directed where someone will notice.

Audible signals are sometimes the best method for alerting others on the ground of your whereabouts and need for assistance. Most recommended by SAR authorities is the athletic-type whistle with a ball inside, because its loud scream carries for miles in open country, it always works, and everyone can use it effectively.

Other audible signals for help can be sent with firearms, with the horn of a stranded vehicle, or just by clacking two stones together. However you send them, remember the internationally recognized signal of threes—a pattern of three gunshots, whistles, or flashes of light sent in quick succession, followed by a long pause, then sent again.

About Animals

The Natural Order of Life in the Wild

Nothing about any wilderness is more fascinating than the many creatures living there, in a world our species no longer recognizes or claims as its own. Every animal, from mosquito to moose, plays a vital, interdependent role in the health of its environment; only we have the distinction of being entirely unnecessary to the natural operation of our own planet.

Having been out of nature's loop since discovering fire, humans often perceive the workings of Creation as harsh, even cruel. But there is no discord in nature, despite appearances. White-tailed deer, for example, are genetically engineered to withstand losing a full third of their population every year, and in fact need to lose that number to maintain a well-fed, disease-free herd. While it's a tribute to our uniquely human sensibilities that we root for the rabbit when a coyote is hot on its tail, in reality the rabbit's death contributes to the overall strength of both species. Utopian human concepts of death don't apply in nature, where death is as important as life, and only the strongest may live long enough to procreate. Predator and prey aren't enemies, but brothers, with each contributing to the overall health and survival of the other.

Wild animals the world over are motivated by three basic instincts—hunger, survival, and sex. These are the forces that drive every species' daily routines in every season in any environment. Most constant among these is the need to eat, and the old Ojibwa proverb, "Find an animal's food and you will find the animal," can be counted as a truism. Only well-fed animals have a chance of surviving predation and the elements to reach breeding age, so the availability of food, be it plant or prey, is key to determining if a species lives in any given area.

Getting close to wild animals demands an understanding of and a respect for their sensory abilities, which in general far exceed our own. It's true that humans see farther into the infrared spectrum, with better color discrimination and sharper long-range eyesight than most animals, but mostly nocturnal forest dwellers have little need for these abilities. Instead, most have evolved sharp close-up eyesight and eyes that see well into the ultraviolet spectrum, which allows them to see as clearly on a black, moonless night as we do in twilight.

Respect especially the incredibly keen sense of smell possessed by almost every species except man. Generally speaking, the longer an animal's nose, the greater the surface area of its nasal passages, and the more scent receptors it will have to send olfactory messages to its brain. Most animals have elongated snouts that deliver environmental data to the brain at a level we humans can scarcely comprehend. They can virtually see with their noses.

Nonetheless, it's easy to defeat a keen sense of smell if you remember always to look and walk into the wind when approaching or hiding at places frequented by wild animals. Scent killers, like N-O-Dor from ATSKO/Sno-Seal (see the source list on page 48), have proved very effective in field trials, but if you hope to observe animals without being detected yourself, approaching any suspected habitat from downwind is always advised.

In a growing number of places where suburban sprawl and new housing are eating away the forest, many species displaced by the sudden removal of their habitats have successfully adapted to life among humans. Deer eat from peoples' gardens; raccoons and opossums raid garbage cans; beavers flood riverfront properties; porcupines eat salty, perspiration-soaked tool handles, and frequently varnished wood siding. The price these animals pay is a greatly retarded sense of smell where humans are concerned. Just as we tend not to notice the unique odors of our own homes, so the constant presence of human spoor in an area makes it tough for animals to differentiate between the scent of a person who was recently there and one who *is* there.

An animal's second strongest line of defense for avoiding potential danger is an acute sense of hearing. As a rule, the larger and more mobile a species' ears, the more directional and sensitive its hearing. Big, constantly swiveling ears allow rabbits to detect and pinpoint the origin of even minute sounds, while squirrels, raccoons, opossums, and other animals that can climb to a safer vantage point have small ears and comparatively poorer hearing.

Again, it's possible for a human to defeat even an acute sense of hearing in the woods, and the most important piece of advice any would-be stalker can take to heart is, Slow down. Except for breeding males actively in pursuit of a mate, no wild animal anywhere is in a hurry to get to any destination, and individuals that put desire ahead of caution typically have short life spans. Only humans travel with a steady, rhythmic pace that stands out against the random natural noises of the wilderness and its slow-moving denizens.

While most animals are nearsighted, all are very quick to notice movement well beyond their range of visual acuity. A sudden flash of motion is sure to be detected by any animal within sight, including sharp-eyed birds, squirrels, and other natural lookouts. As wildlife photographers and other hunters know, defeating the senses of, for instance, a deer also means eluding detection by nature's most vocal tattletales, like red squirrels, blue jays, crows, and a multitude of other species that form the wilderness alarm system. Animals don't communicate directly between species, of course, but over the millennia they've learned to recognize when others are alarmed, and to be alert for the source of that alarm.

Cover scents, odor killers, and camouflage are no defense against birds and squirrels on lofty perches. Nothing passes by these tattletales undetected. But neither do they announce the passing of every animal. Predators like coyotes and bobcats nearly always cause an alarm to be raised, while rabbits and deer pass unmolested. That's largely due to the interest predators show in birds and squirrels as food, while herbivorous prey animals show no interest except when the tattletales sound an alarm.

A predator on the hunt moves differently than a "safe" animal, constantly testing the breeze, looking upward for opportunities, and moving stealthily from one place of concealment to another, pausing at each to listen, smell, and look for prey. Many humans inadvertently emulate these behaviorisms when walking through the woods, alarming an army of small but vocal sentries, which in their turn alert every animal for more than 100 yards in every direction to your presence.

Less likely to trigger this very effective alarm system are humans who move like a deer or a predator whose stomach is full—alert to the surroundings but never looking upward and more or less meandering along without rhythm. Show no obvious interest in the tattletales above, move as if there's no place you have to be, pause every few paces to observe your surroundings, and your passing will raise a minimum of fuss.

Tracking Wildlife

Tracking is a skill that everyone with an interest in wild animals should possess to some degree. By learning to recognize a species' tracks and other sign, you can piece together enough clues left by its passing to form a very good picture of what the animal was, where it had been, where it was going, its size, its diet, and sometimes its sex.

Generic tracking tips include the knowledge that nearly all four-footed animals designed for running walk weight-forward, on the toes, and sometimes their heels print lightly or not at all. Hind prints normally register on top of fore tracks, an almost universal characteristic that allows forefeet to be placed visually, and that precise spot stepped onto by the hind foot on that same side, important when you have four legs in rough terrain. Another trait common to four-legged animals is a little toe on the inside of the foot, opposite our own, and forefeet that are noticeably larger than hind paws. Nearly all four-legged animals run with a "rocking-horse" gait, in which the forelegs print close together and slightly behind more widely separated hind prints.

Tracks At-A-Glance

FRONT

HIND

Deer Family (Cervidae)

Family Species:
White-Tailed Deer (*Odocoileus virginianus*)—shown
Mule Deer (*Odocoileus hemionus*)
Elk (*Cervus canadensis*)
Moose (*Alces alces*)
Caribou (*Rangifer tarandus*)

Family Characteristics:
Cloven hooves front & hind, 2 dewclaws per ankle
Large directional ears
No upper incisors
Males wear antlers most of the year
All species strictly herbivorous

FRONT

HIND

Swine Family (Suidae)

Family Species:
European Wild Boar (*Sus scrofa*)—shown
Domestic Hog

Family Characteristics:
Cloven hooves front & hind, 2 dewclaws per ankle
Generally travel everywhere at a trot
Large snouts for rooting up food plants
Omnivorous diet
Fond of rolling in mud

FRONT

HIND

Peccary Family (Tayassuidae)

Family Species:
Collared Peccary (*Dicotyles tajacu*)—shown
White-Lipped Peccary (*Tayassu pecari*)—S. America

Family Characteristics:
Cloven hooves front & hind, no dewclaws
Generally travel everywhere at a trot
Large snouts for rooting up food plants
Omnivorous diet
Generally dislikes water, but swims well

About Animals 🌲 159

Tracks At-A-Glance

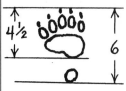

FRONT

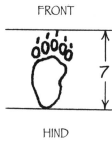

HIND

American Antelope Family (Antilocapridae)

Family Species:
Pronghorn Antelope (*Antilocapra americana*)
Lone survivor of a 20-million-year old family

Family Characteristics:
Cloven hooves resemble those of deer species
No dewclaws streamlines legs for faster running speed
Good vision—some say exceptional
Herbivorous diet of ground plants & prairie grasses
Social, travels in herds of mostly relatives
70 mph running speed, fastest animal in N. America
Black marks on bucks' muzzles lacking on does
Bucks & does grow horns, does usually without prongs

FRONT

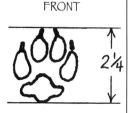

HIND

Bear Family (Ursidae)

Family Species:
Brown or Grizzly Bear (*Ursus arctos horribilis*)
Black Bear (*Ursus americanus*)—shown
Polar Bear (*Ursus maritimus*)

Family Characteristics:
5 toes front & hind feet, small toes innermost
Plantigrade (flat-footed) walk, shuffling gait
Excellent sense of smell, fair hearing, poor vision
Omnivorous diet includes carrion, fish, fruits
Sleep through winter months, but none hibernate
All species superb swimmers

FRONT

HIND

Wild Dog Family (Canidae)

Family Species:
Gray or Timber Wolf (*Canis lupus*)
Coyote (*Canis latrans*)—shown
Gray Fox (*Urocyon cinereoargenteus*)
Red Fox (*Vulpes vulpes*)

Family Characteristics:
4 toes front & hind feet, claws show in tracks
Pointed ears, excellent sense of smell, good vision
Lithe bodies, long furry tails
Both parents take part in rearing young
Pairs believed to mate for life
Mostly carnivorous diet includes carrion, fruits

Wildcat Family (Felidae)

FRONT

HIND

Family Species:

Puma or Mountain Lion (*Felis concolor*)
Bobcat (*Lynx rufus*)—shown
Lynx (*Lynx canadensis*)
Jaguar (*Felis onca*)

Family Characteristics:

4 toes front & hind feet, retractable claws
Lithe, muscular bodies, tail length varies
Excellent sense of smell, fair hearing, good vision
Carnivorous diet includes fish, mammals, fruits
Solitary except when mating, only females rear young
Rarely eat carrion unless starving, prefer to hunt
All cats strong swimmers, but only jaguars like water

Weasel Family (Mustelidae)

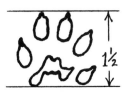

FRONT

HIND

Family Species:

Wolverine (*Gulo gulo*)
Badger (*Taxidea taxus*)
River Otter (*Lutra canadensis*)
Mink (*Mustela vison*)—shown
Ermine (*Mustela erminea*)
Striped Skunk (*Mephitis mephitis*)

Family Characteristics:

5 toes front & hind feet, claws show in tracks
Small toes innermost, may not register in tracks
Perineal (anal) scent glands
Excellent sense of smell, fair hearing, fair vision
Carnivorous diet includes fish, mammals, insects
Slow runners, fierce & willing fighters

Raccoon Family (Procyonidae)

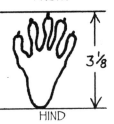

FRONT

HIND

Family Species:

Raccoon (*Procyon lotor*)—shown
Ringtail (*Bassariscus astutus*)
Coatimundi (*Nasua nasua*)

Family Characteristics:

5 toes front & hind feet, small toes innermost
Plantigrade (flat-footed) walk
Long, ringed tail
Omnivorous diet includes meat, fish, insects, fruits
Solitary, mostly nocturnal
Good senses of smell & vision, hearing fair
All species good climbers, ferocious when cornered

Tracks At-A-Glance

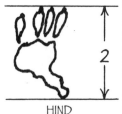

FRONT

HIND

Opossum Family (Didelphidae)

Family Species:
Virginia Opossum (*Didelphis virginiana*)
N. america's only native marsupial

Family Characteristics:
5 toes front & hind feet, thumblike toe on hind feet
Poor vision, fair hearing, excellent sense of smell
Carnivorous diet of mostly carrion, some plants
Solitary except when mating, only females rear
young
Mostly nocturnal, sometimes active by day
Often plays dead when threatened, prefers to tree

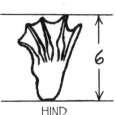

FRONT

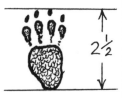

HIND

Beaver Family (Castoridae)

Family Species:
Beaver (*Castor canadensis*)

Family Characteristics:
5 toes front & hind feet
Poor vision, fair hearing, excellent sense of smell
Perineal (anal) scent glands, obvious scent mounds
Strictly herbivorous, eats bark of aspen, willow
Slow runners, very strong & capable swimmers
Always lives on flowing freshwater streams
Social, family colonies of up to 18 animals

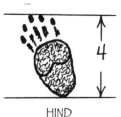

FRONT

HIND

Porcupine Family (Erethizontidae)

Family Species:
Porcupine (*Erethizon dorsatum*)
Single species in N. America

Family Characteristics:
4 toes front, 5 toes hind, unique pebbled soles
Plantigrade (flat-footed) walk
Long, heavily quilled tail
Coarse fur with 30,000 quills on back
Solitary, mostly nocturnal
Good sense of smell, poor vision, hearing fair
Always found in forested areas, cedar swamps

Tracks At-A-Glance

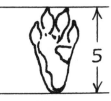

FRONT

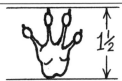

HIND

Hare & Rabbit Family (Leporidae)

Family Species:
Snowshoe Hare (*Lepus americanus*)—shown
Cottontail Rabbit (*Sylvilagus floridanus*)
White-Tailed Jack Rabbit (*Lepus townsendii*)
Black-Tailed Jack Rabbit (*Lepus californicus*)
Nuttall's Cottontail (*Sylvilagus nuttallii*)
Desert Cottontail (*Sylvilagus audonbonii*)

Family Characteristics:
4 toes front & hind feet
Poor vision, fair hearing, excellent senses of smell & hearing
Fast runners, but only for short distances
Herbivorous diet of ground plants, buds, some bark
Solitary, mostly nocturnal
No fixed mating season, breeds prodigiously

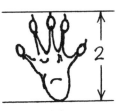

FRONT

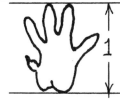

HIND

Squirrel Family (Sciuridae)

Family Species:
Fox Squirrel (*Sciurus niger*)
Gray Squirrel (*Sciurus carolinensis*)—shown
Red Squirrel (*Tamiasciurus hudsonicus*)
Eastern Woodchuck (*Marmota monax*)
Yellowbellied Marmot (*Marmota flaviventris*)

Family Characteristics:
4 toes front, 5 toes hind, elongated hind feet
Good vision, fair hearing, excellent sense of smell
Tree squirrels build cup-shaped nests high in trees
Ground squirrels dig burrows, most hibernate
Herbivorous diet of mostly nuts, some eat insects

FRONT

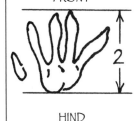

HIND

Muskrat Family (Zibehticidae)

Family Species:
Common Muskrat (*Ondatra zibethica*)

Family Characteristics:
5 toes front & hind, vestigial inner toe
Black, scaly, ratlike tail
Much larger than rat species
Herbivorous diet also includes crustaceans, insects
Solitary, mostly nocturnal
Good sense of smell, poor vision, fair hearing

Recognizing prints is only the first step in learning to track, and while that seems simple enough, most beginners are surprised at how little they actually have to work with. Clear, complete impressions are rare except in mud, wet sand, and fresh snow, so what a tracker follows are not clear footprints but marks made by the animal's passing. Partial tracks—where toes, claws, or the edge of a hoof have pressed noticeably into the earth—can help you identify the species and sometimes the individual, but you might need to follow a trail some distance to get a complete track picture. Of course, you first need to know what a perfect track looks like to recognize partial prints, and the accompanying track identification table provides this information.

Easier to follow and usually more obvious are disturbances left by an animal's feet and body. A half circle of four or five perforations in leafy humus tells you a clawed animal stepped there; twin scrape marks on a moss-covered log show where a deer's hoof slipped; broomlike sweepings on sand denote the wagging of a porcupine's tail as it waddled along; a trough-shaped furrow in grass leading to the water's edge was made by beavers; larger furrows through tall grass tell where a deer or bear crossed; a twisted spiral of crushed grass stems was made when a heavy animal changed direction abruptly by spinning on one foot. Try to imagine yourself as the animal you're trailing, able to slip under low branches or leap over high ones, stopping to nibble a plant here, abruptly changing direction in response to a scent on the breeze.

Trackers who make their job look easy also employ a technique I call looking wide. The trick is to avoid focusing your eyes on the ground, trees, or any single component of the surrounding terrain; instead, take in all of these components as a single picture. Allow your eyes to settle naturally on discontinuities and disturbances left by an animal's passing. You don't need tracks if you can follow a trail. Intersections may still require detective work to discern which prints belong to the animal you're tracking, but a practiced ability to look wide makes following any trail much faster.

Look, too, for territorial marks left by dominant animals advertising their claim to an area, its foods, and any potential mates living there. Most territorial sign is left by dominant males, and all of it is meant to be conspicuous. Bobcats scratch tree trunks with their claws then urinate on the trunks to leave a pungent, distinctly feline aroma that even humans can smell at some distance. Bears leave proportionately larger claw marks on wooden bridges and standing trees, communicating their size and strength to fellow bruins by reaching as high up the trunk as they can. Most territorial animals employ a variety of visual and olfactory markings to attract mates and warn off competitors, usually accompanied by a musky, vaguely skunklike scent that animal watchers should always be alert for.

Animal droppings, known collectively as scat, can also reveal a good deal about their makers, including species, diet, and likely feeding grounds. Territorial predators, from bobcats and coyotes to bears and wolves, use scat to mark the perimeter of their domains, typically leaving fresh scat very near older deposits to refresh their claim every day or so. Members of the deer family evacuate their bowels whenever the urge takes them, usually on well-traveled trails, to disperse their scent widely and to confuse predators. If you can conquer your natural aversion to examining poop, breaking scat apart to reveal its contents will tell you what the animal has eaten and, through deduction, where it was feeding.

Bears (Family Ursidae)

With these generalities in mind let's move on to individual species, starting with bears. No wild animal in North America is more feared by humans, and none has suffered more at the hands of fiction writers seeking to create thrills by painting bears as aggressive, bloodthirsty man killers. Early settlers armed with muzzleloading smoothbores feared these most powerful of land carnivores because of their tremendous strength and sometimes enormous size. Adult brown, or grizzly, bears can exceed half a ton by age five; black bears, which may be black, brown, blond, or even mostly white on Alaska's Gribble Island, can reach mature weights of more than 600 pounds. In either species females are usually about 20 percent smaller than males.

Long canines identify black and brown bears as carnivores, but their feeding habits and lack of hunting prowess classify them as omnivorous, with a diet that consists largely, or at some times of year entirely, of grasses, roots, berries, and other vegetation. Newborn deer fawns and elk or moose calves are frequently stalked along overgrown trails in late spring, and occasionally a hapless ground squirrel is dug from its burrow, but meat is a highly prized delicacy in the diets of both black and brown bears. Polar bears, being adapted to a habitat with almost no vegetation, are almost wholly carnivorous, but their darker-colored brethren normally have to settle for carrion they appropriate from more skilled but less powerful hunters.

Aside from a brief midsummer mating season, or rut, all bears are solitary and concerned only with gaining the layer of fat—about 25 percent of their body weights—they'll need to nourish them through a five-month winter denning period. To accomplish that these large animals must feed constantly, following seasonal foods on an annual trek that might encompass more than 100 miles.

Active mainly from late afternoon to midmorning, bears bed down in secluded thickets to sleep away the warmest part of the day. A nomadic lifestyle makes them less territorial than animals with smaller, permanent domains, but all bears are known to have a "personal space" inside which intruders won't be tolerated.

Few hikers ever see a bear in the midst of prime bear country because both black and brown bears typically withdraw at the first scent or sound of a human, but there are instances where you might suddenly find yourself facing a bear. Approaching from downwind, which is what you'd want to do when stalking deer and other harmless animals, may be a bad idea in bear country. A bear's nose is as sensitive as any, but no animal can

A black bear is identifiable by its rounded head and convex face.

detect scent from upwind. Adding to the ease with which you might catch a bear unawares are small ears with a sense of hearing not much better than our own, and myopic, color-blind vision.

Surprising a bear is never good, regardless of its species. Black bears can be counted on to hightail it into the bushes, and so will most grizzlies, but occasionally there comes a bear that refuses to withdraw. These animals are always large, dominant adults, and nearly always have something worth defending, like cubs, a bee tree, or a deer carcass.

Stumbling onto an obstinate bear doesn't mean you'll be attacked, and even a grizzly mother is reluctant to risk possible injury if she can avoid a fight. The first rule in any surprise encounter with any animal is, Don't run. By running you identify yourself as prey, which may excite the bear's hunting instincts and cause it to give chase. Stand your ground, then slowly back away, never turning your back on the animal until at least 100 yards stand between you. The objective is to convince the bear that you're a potentially dangerous foe, regardless of how untrue that may be, but also that you're willing to withdraw without conflict.

Current bear-avoidance strategy recommends never looking an animal directly in the eye, ostensibly because this conveys a willingness for confrontation. Where more aggressive brown bears are concerned, I must defer to experts like fellow Michigander Doug Peacock, author of the book, *Grizzly Years.* But if the animal is a black bear, an exhibition of anything but total dominance over the beast goes against the teachings of my Indian mentors. I've always locked gazes with every aggressive animal I've encountered, from bears and dogs to moose and elk, and I'll continue using that technique so long as it works.

Be aware, too, that dominant bears especially have been known to charge humans during surprise encounters. Having experienced black bear charges several times, I can attest to the sheer terror inspired by 500 pounds of growling bruin moving toward you at high speed, but once again it's essential that you stand your ground. No human can outrun a bear, but enough have come through bear charges unscathed to prove that nearly every one is a bluff, meant to determine whether you're frightened prey or formidable foe.

Bear tracks are distinctive. Every species has five toes on every foot, each toe terminating in a thick, functional claw. Brown bear claws are long and nearly straight, well suited to digging and inflicting mortal wounds, while black bears have shorter, hooked claws that are better suited for climbing trees to escape brown bears, the black's only natural predator.

Most striking are a bear's hind feet, which look nearly human if you discount claws and the fact that bears, like most animals, walk heavily on the outsides of their feet, so their big and little toes are opposite our own. Tracks are typically toe-in, a trait common to powerfully built, flat-footed (plantigrade) animals not designed for speed, a group that includes badgers, raccoons, wolverines, and humans. At a relaxed walk all four feet usually leave individual prints, with front paws registering slightly behind hind feet on the same side. At a run the forepaws still register behind rear paws, but this time both front and hind feet print in pairs, next to or slightly diagonal to one another. Typical of all running animals, the bear's toes will be dug in more heavily than its heels, often with a spray of loose soil thrown to the rear.

Wild Canids

The family Canidae includes the coyote, gray wolf, gray fox, the imported red fox, and man's best friend, the dog (*Canis domesticus*). There has always been a strong bond between humans and the dog family, and tall tales notwithstanding, no nonrabid wild wolf or coyote has ever posed a danger to humans of any age or size. I've been spending nights alone in the woods with wolves and coyotes since boyhood, and my personal experience has been that any fear of these wild dogs is totally unfounded. Being near these wild hunters, listening to them howl messages across the forest to one another, is a thrill not to be missed.

Coyote (Canis latrans). Coyotes are the most common and widespread wild dogs in the Americas. Smallest of the wolves, coyotes share their long-legged, lanky build, but stand only 24 inches at the shoulder and weigh just 30 to 45 pounds, with males slightly larger than females. At a top running speed of about 45 mph they're natural predators of rabbits and hares, but carrion and rodents—the latter stunned by pouncing onto them with both front paws—make up the majority of any coyote's diet. Fawns and chickens are occasionally taken, but coyotes mostly respect human boundaries, and healthy deer are too much for the little wolf to handle, even in a pack of up to seven adults.

Because a large portion of their diet is rodents, many adults fit the Old West image of a lone coyote, but when winters get tough in the North five to seven adult family members may form a pack to bring down already dying deer. The little wolf isn't keen on tackling prey several times its own size, even with the help of its kin, but deer too weak to use their lethal hooves effectively are sometimes dispatched and eaten quickly, before larger carrion eaters (wolves) find and appropriate the carcass.

Coyotes are normally shy, staying well away from campers and human habitation, although there are places and instances where human practices cause them to become pests. In the late 1950s and '60s, during the paving of California, homeowners who'd settled in what were to become suburbs discovered that local coyotes were smart. They learned not only the milkman's delivery schedules but also how to uncap glass bottles and dump the milk onto concrete—the only nonabsorbent medium available—where it could then be lapped up. Today, as new housing continues to gobble up wilderness, rural homeowners are having similar problems with trash left outside for pickup.

No coyote has ever approached any camp I know of, whether people were there at the time or not, probably due to the shoot-on-sight status coyotes have always enjoyed with hunters. If you should happen upon a pack of coyotes that show reluctance at leaving, say, a fresh-killed fawn, simply brandishing a stick will set the entire pack to running. Be aware, however, that early spring (March and April) is a time when rabies takes a lethal toll on overcrowded animal populations, especially coyotes, raccoons, and skunks. Never, ever approach any wild animal that exhibits no fear, seems disoriented, or has greasy-looking, matted fur. Foaming at the mouth, that classic symptom of hydrophobia (rabies), is seen only at the disease's latter stages, just before the victim dies.

Although such a lightweight and soft-footed animal rarely leaves a clear, whole print, coyote tracks are unique. Like all dog tracks, front and hind prints show four toes with fixed claws, all pointing forward, but the heel pads of the rear feet leave distinctive forward-pointing winged impressions rather like a mustache on each side of their imprints.

Gray Wolf (Canis lupus). It has always seemed a bitter irony that the dog should be considered mankind's best friend while the wolf, which has never been known to attack any human being, has been used to frighten small children and hunted to extinction over most of its range. Native Americans revered the wolf for the way a pack worked together for its own preservation, for the way pairs mated till death did them part, and for the drill-team hunting maneuvers a pack used to bring down prey much larger than themselves. With a running speed of more than 40 mph and body weights that can exceed 140 pounds for males (about 120 pounds for females), wolves running in packs of from two to more than six members are a formidable hunting machine for prey as large as a yearling moose.

In fact wolf and coyote packs are always formed of family members. Some offspring elect not to mate in order to stay with the strength of the pack, where only the original parents, the alpha male and alpha female, are allowed to breed. Offspring that remain for a year or more take an active role as baby-sitters after the next generation of siblings has been weaned, feeding the pups on demand with regurgitated stomach contents and defending them from predation.

But for all their savage efficiency against animals they intend to eat, wolves, like coyotes, pose zero threat to humans, and there is not one verifiable report of a wolf or wolves attacking any human being for any reason at any time in history. I've spent many nights in woods where wolf packs were hunting, listening as they made kills; once I even managed to call an entire curious pack to the perimeter of my camp, but they refused to approach further. Put simply, there is no reason to fear brother wolf.

Wolf tracks can be confusing, even to trained biologists, because they are virtually identical to the tracks of dog breeds that have close ties to their wild cousins. Typical of the dog family, wolf tracks have four forward-pointing toes with thick fixed claws, but the heel pads of front and hind paws may be indistinguishable from those of the husky breeds, like Samoyeds, malamutes, and Siberian huskies. Differences include size, because the tracks of a full-grown gray wolf may reach 5 inches long by 4 inches wide, with front paws larger than hind paws. Note, too, that man's best friend is considered a prey animal by timber wolves. Dog tracks found in wolf country, which is by definition remote, were almost certainly made by a wolf or coyote.

Raccoon (Procyon lotor)

Everyone can recognize a raccoon, with its distinctive masked face, fluffy ringed tail, and long, monkeylike fingers that are notorious for being able to manipulate catches and locks on henhouse doors. The common name stems from the Algonquan Indian name *ah-roo-cown,* which translates roughly to "scratches with hands." *Lotor,* the suffix of its scientific name, is Latin for "washer," an allusion to the omnivorous species' habit of washing food in a stream or pond before eating. The truth is that raccoons, like humans and primates, use their sensitive fingers to separate edible flesh from inedible bones, seeds, and rinds—why eat undigestible matter when you don't have to?

Officially raccoons can reach weights of 12 to 48 pounds, but in the fur-trading days of my youth I took two that topped 60 pounds. Preferred habitat may range from hardwoods to swamp, but always near a source of fresh water, which also provides delicacies like crayfish and clams. They don't hibernate, but in the hardest parts of winter in the Far North raccoons may den for several days at a time, living off stored body fat.

Cartoonists and movie directors have always opted to portray the raccoon as a cute little imp, capable of property damage but always friendly to humans. This simply isn't true. The once popular *Grizzly Adams* TV series was canceled after several youngsters, ostensibly influenced by cute and cuddly trained animal actors, were injured while attempting to handle raccoons drawn to campground garbage cans.

No healthy raccoon has ever attacked a human in my experience, but all are fierce, willing fighters when cornered, and numerous campers have had to endure rabies vaccinations after learning the hard way that a fearless animal isn't necessarily friendly. Raccoon hunters, who typically love their coon dogs like children, are careful to protect their much-larger bluetick, walker, and redbone hounds from the sometimes serious injuries a cornered raccoon can inflict on them. Most feared is that a dog might pursue a coon into deep water, where the raccoon can be counted on to turn and climb onto the stricken dog's head, drowning it. Never approach any wild raccoon, no matter how tame it might appear.

Raccoon tracks are typical of other plantigrade animals, like bears and humans, with elongated hind feet and five toes on each paw. All toes are extraordinarily long, like fingers, and these are perhaps the most distinctive identifying feature of raccoon tracks. Too, remember that nocturnal raccoons always frequent shorelines after dark, and wet sand or mud near the water will often yield plaster-cast-quality tracks.

Beaver (Castor canadensis)

This uniquely American rodent is a marvel of nature. Many Indian cultures credit the beaver with teaching humans to build houses, French voyageurs believed the foul-smelling castoreum glands on the beaver's anus were a cure-all, and no animal in the world does more to promote the health of its own habitat. Today beavers sometimes run afoul of man by flooding power lines and real estate, by toppling commercially valuable birch trees on vacation properties, and by diminishing water flow to cattle farmers on the downstream side of dammed waterways.

In the natural sense, however, beavers do only good: creating ponds and excellent fish habitat where forest once dominated; providing nesting and feeding areas for all types of waterfowl and other birds. Thinning fast-growing trees like poplar, aspen, and birch, the bark of which serves as the beaver's main source of nourishment year-round, promotes new growth and health in the surrounding forest, and every animal in the area will visit the pond to drink at some point every day.

Trees chewed by beavers.

Years later, when the largest food trees are exhausted and the beavers move on to establish new ponds, the abandoned pond will dry up and become a rich garden of lush growth.

Largest of North America's rodents, beavers can officially reach weights in excess of 100 pounds, though 30 to 40 pounds is average for adults. None poses a danger to humans unless cornered on land, but never underestimate a beaver's ability to fight: The famed Lewis and Clark Expedition suffered its first near-fatal casualty when Captain Meriwether Lewis's huge Newfoundland retriever had its throat torn open by a cornered beaver.

Despite a plethora of tracks along muddy or sandy shorelines, easily recognizable beaver tracks are rare. Reasons for that odd scarcity include the fact that beavers seldom walk along a shoreline; instead they travel straight from water to work area, leaving a wide, flattened, furrowlike trail through tall grasses at the water's edge. Webbed hind paws help make beavers among the best swimmers in the mammal world, but print only faintly because of their wide surface area. Fortunately, gnawed trees with bark stripped off, dams, lodges, and, of course, ponds are proof enough that beavers live there.

When tracks are in evidence, there are five toes on every foot, although the small inside toe of the hind feet may not print at all. Front tracks look remarkably like a small human hand with fingers and thumb spread wide. The walking gait is a toe-in waddling pace in which all four feet register independently.

White-Tailed Deer (Odocoileus virginianus)
No wild animal in history has been more studied, manipulated, or revered than the white-tailed deer, and the strangest part is that all the money used to accomplish those things comes from people whose stated goal is to kill deer. Nearly exterminated by the mid–20th century because of unrestricted hunting, whitetails have made a phenomenal comeback, even to the point of becoming agricultural pests and serious driving hazards, especially after dark. Few species have adapted to the crush of civilization better than the whitetail.

Whitetails are one of five native species in North America belonging to the family Cervidae, which also includes mule deer, caribou, elk, and moose. All are ungulates (hoofed animals) of the order Artiodactyla, meaning they have an even number of toes. Other shared characteristics include antlers that are shed by males in winter, cloven hooves, a darker grizzled coat in winter, a purely vegetarian diet, a lack of top teeth, and twins born in early spring.

While I've heard some pretty tall tales from overexcited nimrods, I feel secure in saying that wild white-tailed deer are absolutely harmless to any human. The same applies to mule deer and caribou. Bull elk in the grip of raging hormones during the October rut, or mating season, have been known to charge photographers who got too close, but such instances are rare and roundly deserved. Moose, however, are scary; cows with calves are more protective than any other deer species, and rutting bulls have been known to charge anything up to and including locomotives. Once again, the safest rule of thumb is to give a wide berth to any large deer that seems reluctant to flee at your approach.

Whitetail tracks are typical of deer tracks, printing in the classic split-heart pattern. Each half of the cloven hoof is actually a modified toenail; paired dewclaws located above the hooves to the rear of each ankle are another pair of apparently useless toes that will probably disappear one day. Like those of most four-leggers, hind prints register precisely on top of foreprints at a casual walk. At a fast run of 35 mph whitetails and other deer adopt a rocking-horse gait, with paired foreprints registering between and slightly behind more widely spaced hind prints.

Wildcats (Family Felidae)

Discounting the jaguar, ocelot, and jaguarundi of Mexico, there are three wildcats in North America: the bobcat (*Lynx rufus*), the mountain lion (*Felis concolor*), and the long-legged lynx (*Lynx canadensis*). All are superb hunters with pinpoint hearing, very good vision, and some of the most lethal armament in nature. These cats have the stealth to stalk small rodents, the speed to catch a rabbit, and the teeth and claws to bring down prey much larger than themselves. Unlike wild canids, all cats prefer to kill their own food, and none will eat carrion unless very hungry.

Mountain lions are the largest of American wildcats, reaching weights of more than 250 pounds, followed by the muscular little bobcat at 65 pounds and the long-legged lynx at 40. Each of these was once far more widespread than it is today, but people have never been fond of wildcats in their backyards, and now all of them are more or less cornered in small pockets of wilderness.

While there have been tales of lynx and bobcats attacking humans, I find such stories very difficult to swallow—even a child is physically too large to be considered prey by such small felines. Mountain lions, though, have earned a good deal of prejudice by infrequently killing or mauling small-framed people, sometimes actually eating the bodies. As with bears, the culprits are always old, arthritic cats whose hunting skills are no longer sufficient to supply game. Humans are at the bottom of the list of wildcat food choices.

A chance meeting with a large mountain lion can be frightening. Most will hightail it for cover; if you should meet a cougar that seems reluctant to leave, it probably has a fresh kill or cubs that it's defending. As with a bear, the protocol for safe withdrawal includes maintaining constant eye contact while backing off slowly. Never turn your back on the cat, regardless of what it does, until you've put a minimum of 100 yards between you. Barring this, a blank pistol, a compressed-air horn, or even a loud whistle has always been sufficient to set even large cats to running.

Like canids, all felines have four toes on each foot, but while dogs have paws designed for digging, with stout fixed claws and forward-pointing toes, cats have retractable claws in toes that are arrayed in a semicircle. Cats can partially close their paws like a human fist, and widely spaced toes permit a better grip against flesh while needlelike fangs deliver a killing bite to the victim's throat.

Tracks of the three American wildcats are easily distinguished from one another. Mountain lion tracks are of course much larger and deeper than tracks from its two smaller cousins. Lynx tracks are disproportionately large and show long, widely splayed toes with almost formless heel pads; bobcats are unusual in that all four feet are nearly equal in size, while most animals have larger forefeet. Being retractable, claws are normally absent from the tracks of all species. An exception is on slippery surfaces like wet clay or ice where cats, like people, feel insecure about walking.

10

Weather

The sky was filled with thick, rolling black clouds that swept across the heavens at a disturbing pace as I hurried back to camp. Already the woods had become dark enough to strain my eyes, even though it was still early evening, and the moisture content of the surrounding air was perceptible on my cheeks. Lightning flickered through darkening skies, accompanied by thunderclaps so loud that some caused brief moments of disorientation. I could see a wall of heavy rain coming my way over the darkening northern Michigan hills, and I figured it would be best not to get caught in this one.

I made camp about a half hour before the first marble-size raindrops spattered hard onto the forest floor. By then I'd built and banked my fire against the coming deluge and was rolled snugly inside a sturdy lean-to shelter. Rain began falling in sheets, punctuated regularly with a deafening crescendo of thunder and blinding lightning flashes that nevertheless induced a feeling of deep contentment. I fell asleep.

I hadn't been asleep more than a few minutes when an ear-splitting crash mixed with the sounds of splintering wood popped my eyes wide open—just in time to be blinded by a brilliant flash of white light. Spots danced before me as a ghostly blue haze of electricity made the hairs on my forearms and head stand erect. I knew without looking that a very large tree had fallen much too close to where I lay, wide awake and entirely frightened for the next several hours. I finally fell asleep again sometime before dawn.

I awoke the following morning to clear skies and sunshine so golden that it made me wonder if the previous night hadn't been just a dream. It hadn't. There, not 50 feet behind my shelter, lay a century-old beech tree, its massive trunk twisted and splintered by inconceivable power. I was awed, but mostly I was happy that it hadn't fallen on me.

I dug out my 7-transistor AM radio to see if there would be news about the previous night's weather. It seemed fitting that the first sounds to come from its tinny speaker was Maureen McGovern singing "There's Got to Be a Morning After," the theme song of the then newly released movie *The Poseidon Adventure*.

Weather is the most dangerous threat any of us are likely to face in the woods, and it must never be ignored. As the story above illustrates, lightning is always a potential danger in stormy skies, but it represents just one of many atmospheric hazards that need guarding against.

Identifying Approaching Weather

Weather reports from local radio stations are a woodsman's first and best line of defense, despite inaccuracies, because radar and satellite imaging can detect the approach of storm fronts days before they arrive. Always check the extended forecast for your target area prior to leaving civilization, and try to catch a local weather report every day on your pack radio. Meteorologists are more often right than wrong these days, and when they do err it's usually on the side of harmlessness.

Surprisingly accurate short-term forecasts can be obtained from reading changes in the local environment. The tiny brown pismire ant, whose circular mounds are found along virtually every dirt road, gravel shoulder, and sidewalk crack in North America, will work diligently to close up these mounds when rain is coming. With fair weather on the horizon, the ants' mounds are flattened disks of contrasting sand against the earth, their entrance holes left wide open to facilitate ventilation and constant ant traffic. Changes in humidity and barometric

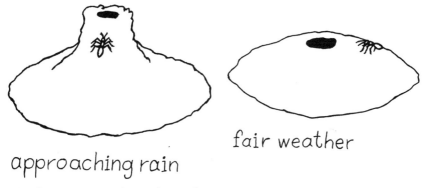

approaching rain

fair weather

Hills of pismire ants can be used to predict an oncoming storm.

pressure warn the insects of impending rain, and workers rush to close nest entrances more tightly against flooding with chimneys of cemented sand that often resemble tiny termite mounds. Occasionally the ants will cry wolf and no rain will fall, but they're never wrong about conditions being favorable for a good shower, and the taller their chimneys, the more likely it is that you're in for a deluge.

Fish behavior can also be an indicator of approaching rain. As air becomes heavier from increased humidity, flying insects hover just inches above the surface of lakes and streams, within reach of trout, bass, and other fish that rise up to eat them with sometimes impressive airborne leaps. Bugs also fly close to water at sunset, attracted by its residual heat, but fish feeding on the surface during the day are a sign that rain is likely.

Birds that feed on flying bugs, like swallows, sparrows, and starlings, take advantage of the calm, heavy air that precedes a rainstorm for the same reason. Their sometimes frenzied feeding, with aerobatics that would put an F-16 to shame, is another sure sign that rain is on the horizon.

To an observant woodsman, the air itself can tell of approaching weather fronts. Probably everyone has heard of the proverbial calm before the storm, even if they haven't actually seen it in person. When birds, cicadas, squirrels, and other normally vocal critters stop their serenades during the day, it's because they've stopped mating, feeding, and feuding to seek cover against approaching weather. In most instances the air will be dead still and the sky overcast, but I've also been surprised by a sudden stillness in the forest on sunny days, usually just minutes before a violent thunderstorm hit.

Be aware, too, that all animals and most insects tend to go silent in the middle of especially hot summer days. Again, this is because they've sought out a cool hole or burrow to sleep away the day's worst heat. In either case a hiker or backpacker is well advised to follow the animals' example.

Clouds offer another option for determining what kind of weather a hiker can expect in the near future. Moving fronts are preceded by winds and clouds moving away from the oncoming weather, and their direction is a good indicator of what type of weather to expect. In probably most places around the world, winds from the north or northwest indicate a cold front moving in, while southerly winds bring warm air. High, thin cirrus or "horsetail" clouds denote cold air; white cotton-ball clouds accompany warm temperatures and fair skies; dirty gray or black cotton-ball clouds mean you should keep shelter close at hand.

Be alert, too, for storm clouds that are moving in a different, even opposite, direction from prevailing winds on the ground, because these may indicate the clashing temperature fronts that can create tornadoes.

Avoiding Weather Problems

Once you've identified approaching weather, the next step is to avoid potential hazards it might bring. The most common weather problem for campers is water in the form of rain. A good rule of thumb for folks who must be out in the rain is to subtract 20 degrees Fahrenheit from the actual temperature, then dress accordingly.

Rain also has a strong influence on where a camp should be placed. If there are hills in an area, be alert for and avoid ravines between them that might serve as natural runoffs. This may be particularly important in high rock country, where a hard rain spread over several square miles of nonabsorbent stone can quickly accumulate into a raging flash flood. A high spot within a small, isolated (not part of a runoff) valley is your best choice in the woods, where most rain is absorbed by spongy humus. In rock country pick a place well to one side and at least 20 feet above suspected drainages.

Lightning

As the anecdote at the start of this chapter illustrates, lightning is also a real concern to people on foot in the great outdoors. The old truism about never taking shelter under a tree during an electrical storm has no meaning in a forest—which is actually one of the safer places to be—but tall trees that extend above the canopy and other high points are to be avoided. Any object projecting above its surroundings, including your body, is a potential lightning rod. Open fields and rocky outcrops are good places to stay away from when the sky starts rumbling.

Tornadoes

As anyone who's lived in tornado or hurricane country can testify, wind is sometimes nature's most frightening force. In the timber country where I grew up, loggers with long life lines were constantly alert for widow-makers—large dead branches and treetops that break off, frequently for no apparent reason, and come crashing earthward with the force of whatever weight they carry. Injuries from widowmakers are actually quite rare, but it wasn't long ago that a 15-year-old boy canoeing Michigan's Au Sable River with his family was killed when a large white birch came apart and crashed down onto his head. Old woodsmen get that way by never disregarding the possibility that a tree will fall in the forest.

In most cases dense lowland forests, like dry swamps, are the safest places to escape Old Man Wind. Air currents that reach them are diminished by surrounding higher ground, and a thick mass of evergreens further diffuses even strong winds to a mere breeze. In these eternally quiet places the real force of a wind is evident in the swaying of tall trees that stand above the surrounding canopy, and these are the very trees a camper should give a wide berth. Trees whose topmost branches receive the full brunt of strong winds routinely snap off, and when the winds reach 50 mph tall trees of any genus can be pushed hard enough to snap off several yards above the ground, bringing perhaps several tons smashing downward. Be especially mindful around large birches, poplars, and aspens, all brittle trees that share a tendency to drop large dead branches.

The upside is that widowmakers are never silent, but the location of a sudden cracking noise overhead might not be immediately apparent. Never stop to look upward, but run to the nearest large tree and wrap your arms tightly around its trunk; this is one instance where being a tree hugger can literally save your life. There, protected by a shield of heavy live branches that grows stronger nearer the ground, you're virtually untouchable by falling wood of any size, even if it falls from the tree you're holding.

Tornadoes are the most frightening and powerful of winds, and in recent years we've seen only too clearly how they can form almost anywhere a warm front collides with a cooler air mass. Flat, open terrain is most conducive to twister formation, but I've experienced three tornadoes in the tall timbered hills of northern Michigan, and the only good thing I can report about any of them was that no one present was injured.

Thick forest offers little protection from the destructive power of a tornado, and nowhere is that power more apparent than in places where twisters have laid miles of strong trees over at crazy angles, brushing them aside like windblown grass. I've noted, however, that cyclones in a woods always follow the path of least resistance, just as they do in open country, and standing timber helps channel this energy more predictably. That means two-tracks and seasonal roads are likely tornado routes, as are riverbeds, valleys, railroad grades, and lakeshores—anyplace that offers a clear avenue for wind to flow. Obviously, these places are to be avoided if you suspect a tornado will form in the area. This almost always means abandoning your vehicle to seek safer cover. If you can pull your car or truck into a nearby narrow valley between two tall hills, this will greatly increase its chances of survival. But such refuges aren't always available, and you're best advised to leave your vehicle in any case.

As always, local weather broadcasts are your best source for up-to-the-minute news about tornadoes, but don't ignore changes in your surroundings that could mean a twister is coming your way. Again, sudden dead silence in the woods, often accompanied by a perceptible clamminess in the air, is always a good indication that rough weather is on the horizon. A warm rain that suddenly turns cold, sometimes bringing sleet or hail, means you're right on the front where a twister might form, and if that rain suddenly goes from vertical to horizontal behind a driving wind, seek shelter immediately.

Most tornadoes occur in the afternoon, when the earth is cooling, but if you hear the trademark freight-train roar at any time of day put at least 200 yards between yourself and likely tornado avenues as quickly as possible. Never try to ride it out inside a building unless it has a basement or cellar, and don't make the obviously foolish but still common mistake of zipping yourself into a tent. Better to lie flat on the ground than to be contained inside anything that catches the wind.

The best strategy for surviving a tornado is to get below the surrounding terrain in a depression too small to be settled into by the microbursts (mini twisters) that always surround a funnel cloud. Large culverts at stream crossings are good places to take shelter, but these may be in short supply. In the woods seek out a small, preferably deep, hollow large enough to accommodate your body and lie flat, facedown, hands locked behind your head until the winds pass. Being in a depression means winds pass over you, while trees snapped off or toppled by them will fall across instead of onto your prone body.

Snow

Snow can be very dangerous to hikers, but while there have been numerous cases of death by exposure, this shouldn't be a concern for modern backpackers who know where they're going and equip themselves accordingly. Of greater concern are subtler and less obvious dangers posed not by the cold, but by the soft, fluffy powder itself.

In places where winter is a season, the worst danger comes from hardpack—a compacted layer of normally permanent snow that covers the ground till spring. This hardpack layer can exceed 4 feet in depth on the level and consist of more than 200 inches of actual snowfall. Fresh powder falls onto this in accumulations that may exceed a foot; these are compacted by their own weight and the warming effect of weak winter sunshine.

In sunless temperatures of 20 degrees Fahrenheit or less, hardpack is usually a pleasure to walk over, because its frozen upper crust is hard as rock. But let a few hours of bleak midwinter sunlight hit that crust and it will turn brittle, too weak to support a human's weight, yet solid enough to force you step down hard with every forward step. This bone-jarring experience can run a trained athlete to exhaustion within a few hundred yards, and it has killed more than a few hunters. A solution I was forced to find one winter during an unseasonable warm spell was, as I noted previously, to pack out to the nearest road during the wee subzero hours of morning, before the rising sun softened the crust too much to support my weight.

The solution, which I recommend for anyone who snowmobiles, hikes, or hunts in snow country, is to wear a pair of quality snowshoes whenever venturing out onto hardpack. Skiers who stick to groomed trails are usually exempt from this rule, but backcountry snowmobilers should always be equipped to hike over long distances. In fresh powder a snowmobile trail can be as tough to walk on as the surrounding snow, crusted just enough to make each step an effort. Throw a track or blow a piston even a couple of miles from civilization under such conditions and you're very much stranded without a pair of snowshoes.

In mountain country you also have to be alert for avalanches, which can bring hundreds of tons of snow sliding downward with sufficient force to wash away buildings and vehicles before settling to layers that might exceed 20 feet. A rule of thumb is that any grade 30 degrees or more above level has the potential for a snow slide in mountain country. (Brunton's 8040 prismatic compass has a clinometer needle for reading grade angles.) Wooded hills are generally exempt from this rule, because so many trees block the way on even steeper slopes, but if several tons of snow gets a start above the tree line, building mass and momentum as it descends, a forest below won't stop it.

The best idea is to give potential avalanche areas a wide berth whenever possible. When this isn't possible, look for places where rippled, rounded layers of snow lying at the bottom of a hill indicate a recent avalanche; these places usually offer safe crossing until the peaks above become snow-heavy again. Be especially wary during or immediately after a heavy snow. Always try to walk on the shaded side of hills to avoid the possibility that sunshine will loosen a slide above you. The same applies in a valley, where either side might pose a danger. If the terrain permits, I recommend trekking 100 yards or so up the shaded side to completely avoid a slide from the opposite, sunny side.

Loose rocks also pose a year-round danger in many places, frequently blocking mountain roads when they avalanche and sometimes bashing unlucky motorists. Beware of all places where loose rock, especially shale, overhangs your trail, and go well around them, even if this means leaving established hiking trails. If you can hear loose stones skittering downward from the force of wind alone, take it as red-hot danger signal and adjust your course accordingly.

11

Man's Rightful Place

Nothing has been more responsible for my lifelong obsession with everything wild than the many Native Americans I knew while growing up in northern Michigan. Teachings from these ancestors of the mighty Ojibwa and Odawa tribes contributed greatly to my perception of nature, of myself, and of life in general. Theirs was a vanishing culture where no knowledge had ever been recorded, but was passed from elder to younger through stories and instruction. Much had already been lost over the half millennium since the gun had supplanted the bow and arrow, but every grandfather felt within himself a traditional duty to preserve what was still remembered by instilling it in the kids.

The grandfathers' problem in those days was that Indian kids from my generation were typically more interested in gaining the trappings of modern society than in learning about the old ways. (I'm happy to report that today both tribes have made good progress in reigniting the interest of youngsters in their respective cultures.) It was probably out of sheer desperation for an interested student that the old-timers accepted a headstrong Irish kid who had no birthright to their teachings. Their misfortune has become my blessing.

The lesson I most thank my Native American mentors for is the one that allows me to view the world through Indian eyes. No humans have ever understood their real place in nature and on earth better than Native Americans. Their social structure, beliefs, and religion were formed by the world around them, a world in which they realized they were but a small, mostly insignificant part.

I heard many stories about the People from a grandfather named Amos Washageshik, a full-blooded Ojibwa who still spoke his native tongue easily and spent as much time out-of-doors as possible. Every evening you could find him seated on an upturned bucket in front of a small fire in his front yard, where he'd remain until it was time for bed. Even in winter he found the flames of his small fire preferable to the warmth of a furnace-heated house. Adults who weren't enemies were welcome to join him, and many did, but it was the children he regaled with lessons in woodcraft and stories of his ancestors.

As Amos told it, in the beginning Manitoba (God) created the earth and all its animals, and all things were designed to live in harmony with one another, each of them more or less critical to the existence of all others. Only God could have made such an incomprehensibly complex global ecosystem, but even He couldn't be in every part of His vast kingdom at the same time. He needed intelligent creatures who could serve as guardians, watchers of remote worlds, reporting directly to Him.

So Manitoba created the Nish-Na-Bee, the People, a single tribe with a single tongue that today has grown to cover the planet in a variety of races and languages. They were strange, naked creatures who walked upright and were neither angel nor animal, but something between. Their single purpose was to provide information to Manitoba, and toward that end only they among all creatures were endowed with an ability to communicate directly to Him through the gift of prayer.

The People's design made them slow and clumsy by animal standards, but as the eyes and voice of Manitoba on earth they were meant to be conspicuous reminders to all that God's protection was never far away. In those early days of mankind all creatures were united by a single spoken language, so animals for which the world was created could report matters needing the attention of God to a guardian human. As the eyes of Manitoba, Nish-Na-Bee were intended to work between sunrise and sunset, when the Creator's presence is strongest, and they were given superior daytime eyesight. At night, when People were expected to sleep so they might better receive visions—instructions from God—they were all but blind.

Though People, like all of their brethren, were of the earth, they were not permitted to take a direct role in its function. To help ensure this, they were denied good senses of smell and hearing, claws, and fangs, lest their God-given intelligence make them too powerful as hunters. They were allowed to take the bodies of their brother animals for nourishment, but People alone bore a responsibility to explain through prayer why they'd released a soul to Manitoba. As guardians of earth, they possessed a knowledge of right and wrong not present in the animals, and so only they were capable of sin. To kill for need was a sacred act, and if a hunter was worthy his prey would offer itself willingly. Upon taking possession of the carcass, whether a frog, fish, or deer, the animal's spirit and Manitoba were both thanked through prayer. Blessed were hunters who gave of themselves for the benefit of others, but no sin was greater than killing without need.

Lessons of life were passed along to younger generations most often in the form of a story. Unlike European fairy tales, which have but one moral at their ends, Indian fables are intended to make the listener think, and there are always several lessons to be gained from a single story. I can't hope to relate these stories with the same magic they had when told by a man who was born when today's highways were wagon trails, but now that I'm a grandfather, I too have a duty to pass them along in the best way I can.

Legend of the Red-Winged Blackbird

No migratory bird is more a harbinger of spring's warmth than the red-winged blackbird (*Agelaius phoeniceus*). Every spring these birds return north in great armadas to reclaim the marshes where generations of them have spent each summer since time immemorial, driving the icy grip of winter from the land with their distinctive song. At this time the black males, with their bright red and yellow wing patches, can be seen clinging to upright cattail stalks, calling for less conspicuous brown-speckled females with a warbling "cure-eeeee." With remarkably little fear of humans, red-winged blackbirds adorn the marshes throughout summer, mating, rearing young, molting, and then flying to warmer climes before winter again sets its claws into the land.

To the Ojibwa, the red-winged blackbird was one of several sacred animals, and legend has it that a male blackbird once saved the earth from destruction by fire. It happened in the time when People were new to the world and every creature shared a common language. There was but one tribe then, with a single chief, appointed by Manitoba to keep His laws among the People. Humans had the freedom to do as they pleased, so long as they refrained from harming one another and the world, for doing either was an affront to God that would not go unpunished.

But even Manitoba didn't foresee how the intelligence He'd bestowed upon His guardians of earth could evolve from simple ingenuity into avarice, envy, and a lust for power. Soon the sins of selfishness and temptation began to emerge. Those who refused to respect tribal law were banished from the tribe, the most terrible punishment a Person could receive, and were made by God to speak a different tongue as evidence to all of their crimes against nature.

The first Person ever ejected from the One Tribe was a great hunter named Black Fox. The Nish-Na-Bee had already been on earth for as many seasons as there were stars, and the light of life had begun to fade in the old chief's eyes, as God had ordained it must eventually fade in all of His children. As reward for his long service to Manitoba and the wisdom with which he'd ruled, the old chief was allowed to choose his own successor from among the smartest and strongest young men of the tribe. Animals and birds carried word throughout the world that all braves were to return to the village for the choosing.

Black Fox was a hopeful contender, and he knew that he had every reason to be confident. No hunter in the tribe could match his hunting and tracking skills, and few had ever bested him in a wrestling match. His downfall was that he very often achieved victory through trickery and deceit.

All the young men felt both exhilaration and terrible sadness as they waited outside the dying chief's tepee for his decision. When an elder finally emerged to announce his choice, there was a moment of great joy and many embraces for Running Wolf, the new chief.

Black Fox was incensed. How dare the tribe discount his hard work and the many contributions he'd made for the good of all? Running

Wolf would make a fine chief, to be sure, but Black Fox was unable to see that a leader of the people needed not just skill in the forest but also compassion and understanding for all of God's children.

Black Fox spent a sleepless night struggling with thoughts of vengeance, an overwhelming emotion that he'd never felt before. He arrived at a plan in the gray light of predawn, and slipped silently from the sleeping village. His anger grew as walked, and when he stopped at midday a great evil had taken possession of his will.

All of earth was a vast forest in that age, and it was Black Fox's plan to start a fire large enough to consume the whole world. His thoughts were clouded by images of revenge as he worked his drill ever faster against the fireboard. A plume of white smoke rose from the tinder pile, and he blew it into a flame with practiced skill, then piled on deadwood as quickly as it would burn.

So engrossed was he in thoughts of retribution that Black Fox failed to notice a blackbird that flew in to watch the unusual proceedings. Not as intelligent as his larger cousin the crow, the blackbird was no less curious, and even he was smart enough to know when something was out of the ordinary.

"Black Fox," the bird said, startling the brave from his vengeful imaginings, "why do you build such a large fire? The sun is warm, and you have no meat to cook."

Filled with an unexpected guilt about his horrific plans, Black Fox turned on his small brother in anger. "Go away, stupid bird," he shouted. "You have nothing to say about what I do." He picked up a stone and threw it at the startled blackbird, narrowly missing.

Shaken at being treated so by a guardian, and sensing finally that something was seriously amiss, the bird persisted until Black Fox's anger erupted in a spew of words and he revealed his awful plan.

The little blackbird was horrified. "I'm going to tell the People what you're doing," he cried, rising on all-black wings. "They will have a cure for your madness."

Black Fox's anger turned to fear when he imagined what the tribe's reaction would be to this nosy blackbird's announcement, and his first impulse was to stop them from learning his secret. A second stone flew from his hand, and this time the aim was to kill. The missile struck hard against blackbird's wing, knocking the hapless messenger from the air.

The stunned bird lay on the ground, a bright red bloodstain spreading outward from where the stone had impacted his shoulder.

With a savage cry, Black Fox leaped forward to end his small victim's life. But Manitoba had used the heart of an eagle to make a blackbird; this one summoned all his strength and rose out of reach on bloodied wing before the brave could make good on his murderous intentions.

On and on the injured bird flew, struggling hard against pain and weakness to stay airborne on his bleeding wing until he reached the Nish-Na-Bee village. Several times he was forced to rest, and every pause only made it harder to rise up again on broken wing and continue onward. The sun had begun to set when the heroic little bird finally burst upon the Nish-Na-Bee village crying, "Cure-eeeee, cure-eeeeeeee."

Upon hearing the exhausted blackbird's tale, the new chief, Running Wolf, selected 100 of his strongest braves (there was no war then, and so no warriors) to accompany him, and left the village to stop Black Fox. The rogue tribesman was found and bound with braided rawhide—the first human ever taken into custody—but his fire had grown beyond the Nish-Na-Bee's ability to control. Prayers to Manitoba brought a deluge of mighty thunderstorms that extinguished Black Fox's foolish attempt at arson as easily as a man stamps out a cinder.

Since no crime could be more heinous than one whose intent was to harm the land on which all things depended, Black Fox's punishment was swift and harsh. With a heavy heart, Manitoba decreed that Black Fox and all of his descendants be banished forever to the Far North, where winters can kill and firewood is prized for being scarce. There they would learn to appreciate the splendors of a warm fire and hot food while competing for game with the great white bear, which even today considers People as prey. It should have been a death sentence, but the repentant Black Fox and his wife thrived in that hostile land, establishing their own tribe but losing forever the ability to speak with animals.

The little blackbird recovered fully under the tender care of tribal women, and was rewarded for his bravery with the highest of honors: a badge that would be worn forever by his ancestors to remind them of the day one small blackbird saved the world from fiery destruction. The badge was colored red and yellow, the colors of fire, and was to be worn on each wing in the same spot as the original wound. The heroic little blackbird was proud and honored, but since that day all red-winged blackbirds fear fire and are never found far from water.

Ursa Major and Ursa Minor

Probably everyone who's looked into a night sky can recognize the Big and Little Dippers, known respectively to astrologers as Ursa Major and Ursa Minor because with a little imagination you can make out the figures of a large and a small bear.

The Ojibwa have a legend about these bears and how they achieved their heavenly positions. The story takes place in Michigan's Upper Peninsula on the Straits of Mackinac, near what is now St. Ignace. It had been a lean summer for bears, so a young sow black bear and her year-old cub set out to find a place where living was easier and food more plentiful. The longer she studied the far side of the straits, 5 miles distant, the more enticing seemed its lush shoreline, rich with the promise of more food than two bears could ever eat.

All bears are powerful swimmers, so mother and cub entered the gently lapping waters between Lakes Michigan and Huron with confidence, paddling easily and swiftly southward. The cub kept pace with his mother until midstream, where swift, powerful currents and strong undertows slowed their progress to a snail's pace. The cub began to tire and was frequently washed under by strong, windblown waves. Excepting humans, all of Manitoba's children have been spared the burden of tears, so the mother continued onward as she knew she must while the cub's small body disappeared forever under whitecapped waters. There was a new hunger in her heart to birth and rear another baby, but God has seen to it that animals, which are incapable of sin, bear no sorrow that might harm their chances of survival.

Alone now, the sow continued her struggle against the treacherous Mackinac waters. Both she and her cub had been hungry when they'd started the crossing, and now even her powerful body was tiring fast, drained of available fuel. The sun sat low on Lake Michigan when the bear's courageous determination finally brought her free of the currents and into calmer water. There, within sight of the southern shore, the sow's flesh and bones found their limits and ceased to function, even though her determination never flagged. Protesting loudly against this injustice, the paralyzed bear sank under gentle waters forever.

Having already claimed the cub's freed soul, Manitoba was aware of the young sow's valiant struggle against impossible odds, but would not intervene in nature's course. He was greatly impressed by her courage and strength, however, and spared her from death. A tremendous flash lit the universe, and both bears were placed forever in the heavens, where their ancestors have ever after used them to guide their footsteps at night.

Bearwalks

When I was a boy, I often heard Indian adults talking about bearwalks—nights when free-roaming spirits, some of them bad, were allowed to take earthly bodies. Being the guardians of Manitoba, People not already insane or evil were exempt from occupation by these spirits, so they usually possessed the next most powerful creatures, bears. On such nights the normally solitary bears would travel centuries-old footpaths to congregate in secret spiritual meeting places. One of these places was said to be Greensky Hill, an Ojibwa cemetery near Charlevoix, Michigan, where many people claimed to have seen large groups of bears gather at twilight. According to legend, spirits possessing the bears had until dawn to complete whatever earthly tasks they needed to accomplish, and they were allowed to borrow the form of any animal. Many remained as bears, but some found it more advantageous to become an eagle, wolf, or some other animal.

The Indians didn't fear such spiritual wanderings but accepted them as a part of the natural world that lay beyond the range of their senses, like the hearing of a coyote or a deer's sense of smell. They did, however, believe that strange and sometimes dangerous things happened on these nights.

Isabel was a squat, middle-age Ojibwa woman who seemed to attract bearwalk spirits, perhaps because she also seemed to have an acute sensitivity to things beyond normal human perceptions. One night when I was 10, I overheard her tell my mother that tonight there would be a bearwalk, she could feel it in her bones. Her prediction proved frighteningly correct.

Our farmhouse sat several miles out of town on a remote dirt road, and in 1966 we were among many rural families that didn't have a telephone. My stepfather and uncle were gone on a weeklong trucking run, taking our one vehicle with them, so we were pretty much isolated from civilization.

About midnight, when my younger siblings and I were in bed, my mother and Isabel were sitting on the farmhouse's roofed fieldstone porch enjoying the quiet, warm night air. Suddenly a swarthy man appeared from the shadows in the direction of the barn and demanded entrance into the house. My mother, who never weighed more than 100 pounds, refused. When she moved toward the door, and the loaded .22 rifle inside, the man stepped up onto the porch and threw an arm around her, dragging her back.

His mistake was ignoring Isabel, who'd grown up pulling stumps and rocks with mules in the timber country of northern Michigan. She dealt the surprised assailant a tremendous blow that knocked him through the wooden porch rail. Hurt and enraged, the man leaped to his feet and threw Isabel to the ground, then again headed for my mother, who was frozen in fear.

But before he could reach her, a bushel-size fieldstone arced through the air to thud hard against his lower back. The man fell to his knees, then rolled onto his side in a fetal position, obviously in great pain. Isabel gave him a few hard kicks to maintain that elevated pain level while my mother, who had come to her senses, ran for a gun. Incredibly, the man rolled off our porch, got to his feet, and fled into the darkness, never to return.

Isabel firmly believed that strange man who emerged from the shadows miles from the nearest paved road was not a man at all but a powerful bearwalker spirit that had assumed human form, perhaps possessing someone already a little insane. I don't know if she was right, but she did predict that spirits would be roaming that night. I'm just glad she was there.

God's Knife

Members of the deer family have always played a critical role in the development of native cultures around the world. Having found themselves in the category of prey, moose, elk, caribou, and white-tailed and mule deer adapted to become masters of this role. Few predators except humans can pose a threat to healthy adults, while a reproductive system geared to compensate for a 33 percent herd loss annually ensures an abundance of young bucks and does.

But just as night is vital to day, so is death a critical component in the life cycle of every earthly creature. The Nish-Na-Bee, who would not kill without need, took but a fraction of the deer replaced through birth each spring, so herds thrived. In time the growing number of animals had all but stripped browsing areas bare, which meant that none of them received adequate food. In their weakened state they became susceptible to disease and injury, and great numbers began to die the following winter.

Since the well-being of the People was inextricably tied to that of the deer, tribal elders viewed the increasing number of carcasses with dismay. Fearful of starvation for themselves, the elders turned to Deer Woman, a wise old grandmother whom Manitoba Himself had made spirit sister of the deer. Deer Woman told them of a vision visited upon her by God, which showed a great black infection had settled onto her namesakes. The vision instructed her to travel far north to a sacred spring, where she would find God's Knife, a tool for cutting away the disease and restoring the deer herds to health.

The next morning Deer Woman set out alone through swirling snow to visit the sacred spring, finally reaching it after a walk of many days. There, through a hole in the ice, she could see movement beneath the water. With great faith in God, she plunged her arm into the frigid spring and pulled a large, furry animal onto the snow. A second grab through the ice produced an identical but slightly smaller specimen.

Deer Woman studied the gifts she'd received. The animals had thick fur coats to ward off the cold, long, lanky legs that identified them as fast runners, senses that rivaled a whitetail's, and strong, sharp teeth with powerful jaws. At first she was afraid to be near predators so well designed for killing, but Manitoba made her understand that His Knife, which He named wolf, would never harm a human, a promise that has not been broken to this day.

The wolves were swift, efficient, and terrible in their appointed duties. Working as if with one mind, the pair, which soon grew to a pack, probed deer herds for any sign of injury or weakness. By God's design, no healthy adult deer had need to fear brother wolf, but deer suffering along the trail to death, and offspring born too weak to live as they were meant to, were sent quickly to the Great Spirit. Before long only healthy, strong deer were left in the herds. Since then deer and wolves have been brothers, needing one another to ensure the health and survival of their own kinds.

Index

A

Abrasions, 98–100
Antelopes, American, tracks of, 160
Ants
  as food, 143
  in weather, 178–79
Avalanches, 184

B

Backpacks, 26–29
  packing, 66–68
  sources for, 48–52
Bears, 165–68
  tracks of, 160
Beavers (Castor canadensis), 172–73
  tracks of, 162
Bees, 68–69
Big dipper
  legend of, 191–92
Blackberry, highbush (Rubus
  allegheniensis), 122
Bobcat (Lynx rufus), 174–75
Bonesets, 122–23
Boots
  hiking, 17–21
  sources for, 48–52
  winter, 22–25
Bowline knot, 145
Bugs, 68–69
  bites, treatment of , 103–04, 110
  repellents for, 73–74, 110, 114,
    126

Burdock, common (Arctium minus),
  111
Burns, 95–96, 103

C

Campfires, 76–79
  bow–and–drill starter for, 148–51
  building techniques for , 134–36
  cooking at, 85–89
  starting kits for, 5–7
Campsite
  avoiding problems at, 180
  organization of, 84
  selection of, 75–76
Canteens, 80–81
Caribou, 174
Catnip (Nepeta cataria), 125–26
Cattail, broadleaf (Typha latifolia),
  117–19
Clothes
  drying of, 83–84
  sources for, 48–52
Coal bed, 136–37
Compasses, 2–5, 53–54
  chronograth–type watch, 62
  map, 56–60
  prismatic, 60
  sources for, 48–52
Coon, Nelson
  Using Plants for Healing, 125
Coyotes (Canis latrans), 168–69
Cudweed, fragrant (Gnaphalium
  obtusifolium), 123–25

Cuts, 98–100
Cyclones, 181–83

D

Deer
    legend of, 193–95
    mule, 174
    tracks of, 159
    white–tailed (*Odocoileua
        virginianus*), 173–74
Dehydration, 100–01
Dogs, wild
    tracks of, 160
Double half–hitch slipknot, 144–45

E

Elk, 174
Emergencies
    medical, 98–108
Equipment
    organization of, 84
    packing of, 66–68
    sources for, 48–52

F

Fern, bracken (*Pteridium aquilinum*),
    116–17
Fires
    bow–and–drill starter for, 148–51
    building techniques for, 134–36
    campfires, 76–79
    cooking, 85–89
    starting kits for, 5–7
Fisherman's knot, 146
Fly–poison (*Amianthium
        muscitoxicum*), 113
Foods, 89–91
    natural, 142–43
    See also specific plants
Frogs, as food, 143
Frostbite, 101–02

G

Garlic, 112–14
Giardia lamblia, 115, 138–39, 142
    remedy for, 127
Global Positioning System (GPS),
    3–5
Gloves, 25–26
    sources for, 48–52
Goldenrod, tall (*Solidago altissima*),
    111–12
Grizzly Years, 167
Grubs
    as food, 142

H

Hares
    tracks of, 163
Hut, debris, 131, 133–34
Hydrophobia, 169
Hypoglycemia, 106–08
Hypothermia, 102–03

I

Insects, 68–69
    bites, treatment of, 103–04, 110
    repellents for, 73–74, 110, 114,
        126

J

Jewelweed, common (*Impatiens
        capensis*), 72, 120–21
Joe–Pye weed, sweet (*Eupatorium
        purpureum*), 122–23

L

Lean–to, 131–32
Leek, wild (*Allium tricoccum*),
    112–14
Lifesaving techniques, 146–52
Lightning, 181

Little dipper
    legend of, 191–92
Lynx *(Lynx canadensis)*, 174–75

M

Maps, 54–55
    compass, 56–60
Moose, 174
Moss
    growth of, 61
Moss, reindeer *(Cladina rengiferina)*,
    119–20
Mountain lion *(Felis concolor)*,
    174–75
Muskrats
    tracks of, 163

N

Native Americans
    legends of, 185–95
    origins of Ojibwa, 186–87
Navigation, 53–64

O

Ojibwa
    origins of, 186–87
Onions, 112–14
Opossums
    tracks of, 162

P

Pace counter, 58–59
Parasites, waterborne, 115, 138–39,
    142
    remedy for, 127
Peacock, Doug
    Grizzly Years, 167
Pearly everlasting *(Anaphalis
    margaritacea)*, 123–25
Peccary, tracks of, 159
Pillows, 81–82

Pit vipers, 70–71
Plantain, common *(Plantago major)*,
    110
Plants
    harmful, 71–72
    medicinal, 110, 120, 122–27
Poison ivy *(Toxicodendron radicans)*,
    71–72, 121
Poison oak *(Toxicodendron
    diversiloba)*, 71–72
Porcupines
    tracks of, 162

R

Rabbits
    tracks of, 163
Rabies, 169
Raccoons *(Procyon lotor)*, 171–72
    tracks of, 161
Radios
    receivers, 39–40
    transceivers, 40–42
Red–winged blackbird
    legend of, 187–91
Reindeer moss *(Clandina
    rangiferina)*, 119–20
Roasting spit, 87–88

S

Sandals, 22
    sources for, 48–52
Shelters, 130–34
    sources for, 48–52
    tents, 34–37
Signals
    emergency, 152–54
    mirrors, 153–54
Sleeping
    bags, 29–33
    bag warmers, 80–81
    coal bed, 136–37
    pads, 33–34

pillows, 81–82
platform, 79–80
Snakes, 69–71
  bites, treatment of, 104–06
  as food, 142–43
Snares
  setting of, 151–52
Snow
  blindness, 100
  dangers of, 183–84
  dugout, 134
Snowshoeing, 44–47
  in emergencies, 146–48
  sources for, 48–52
  techniques of, 47–48
Socks, 15–17
  sources for, 48–52
Sprains, 106
Square knot, 144
Squirrels
  tracks of, 163
Stalking
  techniques of, 155–65
Stinging nettle (Urtica dioica), 72
Sumacs, 71–72
Survival
  McDougall's Laws of, 130
  skills for, 146–52
Swine
  tracks of, 159

T

Tansy, common (Tanacetum vulgare),
  126–27
Timber hitch knot, 145
Tornadoes, 181–83
Tracking
  techniques of, 155–65
Triangulation, 59–60
Two–way radio, 40–42

U

Ursa Major and Ursa Minor
  legend of, 191–92
Using Plants for Healing, 125
Utensils, 91–93

V

Violets (Viola spp.), 115–16

W

Wasps, 68–69
Watches
  chronograph–type, 62–63
Water, 137–39
  condensation still, 140–41
  parasites in, 138–39, 142
  portable filters, 12–14
  purification of, 139–42
  sanitation of, 139
Watercress (Nasturtium officinale),
  114–15
Weasels
  tracks of, 161
Weather
  changes in, 178–80
  problems in, 180–83
  radios, 39–40
Wildcats, 174–75
  tracks of, 161
Winds, 181–83
Wolf, gray (Canis lupus), 170–71

Y

Yellow jackets, 68–69